PARTH DAMA

Money, Tech, and You

A Young Person's Guide to Fintech, Cryptocurrency, and AI in Finance

Copyright © 2024 by Parth Dama

All rights reserved. No part of this publication may be reproduced, stored or transmitted in any form or by any means, electronic, mechanical, photocopying, recording, scanning, or otherwise without written permission from the publisher. It is illegal to copy this book, post it to a website, or distribute it by any other means without permission.

Parth Dama asserts the moral right to be identified as the author of this work.

Parth Dama has no responsibility for the persistence or accuracy of URLs for external or third-party Internet Websites referred to in this publication and does not guarantee that any content on such Websites is, or will remain, accurate or appropriate.

Designations used by companies to distinguish their products are often claimed as trademarks. All brand names and product names used in this book and on its cover are trade names, service marks, trademarks and registered trademarks of their respective owners. The publishers and the book are not associated with any product or vendor mentioned in this book. None of the companies referenced within the book have endorsed the book.

First edition

This book was professionally typeset on Reedsy.
Find out more at reedsy.com

Contents

1. Introduction   1
2. The Evolution of Finance   5
3. Fintech   16
4. Blockchain and Cryptocurrency   26
5. Artificial Intelligence and Machine Learning   35
6. Mobile Banking   42
7. Investing in the Digital Age   58
8. The Future of Finance   69
9. Regulatory Challenges in Fintech   80
10. Sustainable Finance and ESG Investing   87
11. Cybersecurity in Finance   93
12. Algorithmic Trading and Hedge Funds   102
13. Behavioral Economics in Finance   109
14. Emerging Trends in Payments   116
15. Risk Management in the Digital Era   124
16. Navigating Career Paths in Finance and Technology   136
17. Conclusion: Shaping the Future of Finance with Technology   143

1

Introduction

Welcome to Money, Tech, and You: A Young Person's Guide to Fintech, Cryptocurrency, and AI in Finance. This book shall be your guide to understanding how technology is changing the landscape of finance and what that means for you. It doesn't matter if you dream of being a financial whiz or a tech-savvy entrepreneur, or you just wish to know how to manage better the money you have to live a more effective life; this guide is meant to set you on that exciting path where finance and technology meet.

The world of finance is experiencing tumultuous change, with new technologies at the forefront of defining savings, investment, consumption, and money management. Thus, The young have access to an unprecedented level of ease, efficiency, and personalization in financial services—from mobile banking apps to cryptocurrencies. With the increasing evolution of technology, young people must get to be in tune with such changes and what they imply.

Now imagine a world in which you handle all your finances only with a smartphone, investing in companies on the other side of the world with just a few clicks, or paying for that morning coffee with a cryptocurrency. But this is not a world tomorrow; it's here today. Understanding these changes will take you not just towards making better decisions about your finances but will also open up new opportunities in innovation and paths in your career.

This book is organized by some chapters on the various features the financial industry's transformation takes. We will first look at the history of finance and how it has evolved into what it is today. From that point, we will jump into the realm of fintech, blockchain and cryptocurrency, artificial intelligence, and more. Along the way, we will consider current and future benefits, issues, and implications from these technologies.

Financial literacy is vital at this moment. Growing up, you will be faced with quite several money-related choices ranging from how to manage your allowance, save for college, credit cards, and make an investment for the future. Being financially literate fundamentally implies that a person has the knowledge and the necessary skills to make sound decisions regarding their money. It is a sad fact that most individuals have the minimum understanding concerning finance, leading to incorrect financial decisions with more prolonged implications. Understanding finance and technology already puts you ahead on the road to success. You'll be able to navigate confidently in the financial landscape, easily avoiding the potholes and moving toward new vistas.

Exploring the world of finance and technology makes it necessary to understand the functions of regulatory bodies and government intervention. The role played by these institutions ensures that financial markets provide a smooth and level playing field, safeguarding the interests of consumers and maintaining economic stability. Some regulations can also influence how new technologies are accepted and integrated into the system. For instance, most governments in the world are currently wondering what type of regulations will be put in place to regulate cryptocurrencies to stem fraud and protect the investor. Information on these regulatory frameworks will expose you to a better view of the financial industry and how it is run.

Economic history has it that economic crises were key drivers in defining

INTRODUCTION

the evolution of finance. Events like the Great Depression, the 2008 financial crisis, and more recent economic shocks have furthered changes in regulations, monetary practices, and public perceptions of the financial system. We shall learn much concerning risk management, economic resilience, and notably the role of supervision from studying these crises. Lessons are pertinent in that they reveal challenges and opportunities that surface in doing business in a dynamically changing world of finance.

Globalization has interlinked the world's economies and their financial markets. Financial decisions taken today in one part of the globe can have worldwide repercussions. The net result of these has been a series of benefits that have accrued to investors in terms of new opportunities for investment and economic growth, with new complexities and risks. Understanding the effect of globalization on finance will make you appreciate a broader horizon under which financial decisions are made. It shall also underscore the international collaboration and regulation required to keep a world economy robust and thriving.

All these would not been possible without extensive innovation at the heart of the change in finance. From the creation of the credit card to the development of online banking, innovation in finance has continuously spurred change and brought improvements in managing our money. This book has most of the inspiring innovations that are happening in finance, such as peer-to-peer lending, robo-advisors, and digital currencies. We also discuss what the future potential innovations will be that might launch this industry into the next revolution.

The world of finance is complex and ever-changing, but it also allows opportunity for anyone with the will to learn and adapt. By acquainting yourself with more knowledge on the technological advancements shaping the industry, you will be in a better position to make well-informed decisions regarding the new opportunities and challenges coming your way. As you read this book, I urge you to remain curious and open-minded. The future of finance is still being written, and as a young person, you have the power to shape it. Now, in exploring the electrifying world of cash, tech, and you, let's do this together.

Introducing cryptocurrencies into contemporary finance has thrown in an entirely new dimension. A shadowy individual or group issued the first cryptocurrency called bitcoin, Satoshi Nakamoto, in 2009. What has been so revolutionary about Bitcoin is that no intermediary, for example, a bank—hence a virtual currency—is controversial and revolutionary at the same time. Other cryptocurrencies that have followed include Ethereum, Litecoin, and Ripple, each offering its unique features and applications.

2

The Evolution of Finance

The 1980s and 1990s witnessed a wave of financial deregulation, globalization, and technological advancement. Financial markets became increasingly interconnected, and new financial instruments, such as derivatives, emerged. The rise of the internet transformed how financial services were delivered, enabling online banking, trading, and investment.

The story of money and finance is as old as human civilization itself. From the barter systems of ancient times to the sophisticated digital transactions of today, the way we manage and exchange value has undergone profound transformations. Understanding this evolution is crucial for appreciating how technology continues to drive change in the financial industry.

In the earliest days of human society, people relied on barter to exchange goods and services. If a farmer had surplus grain and needed tools, they would trade with a blacksmith who needed food. While barter allowed for direct exchanges, it was highly inefficient. The lack of a common medium of exchange made transactions cumbersome and limited the ability to store and measure value.

The advent of money transformed this system. The earliest forms of money were commodities like shells, livestock, and precious metals, which had intrinsic value and were widely accepted as a means of exchange. These commodities served as a more efficient medium, enabling people to trade more easily and accumulate wealth.

As societies grew more complex, so did their economic systems. The development of coinage around 600 BCE in Lydia (modern-day Turkey) marked a significant milestone. Coins, made from precious metals like gold and silver, were durable, portable, and divisible, making them ideal for trade. They also featured standardized weights and government seals, which authenticated their value.

As commerce expanded, the need for secure storage and management of money became evident. Temples and palaces initially served as depositories for wealth, but over time, specialized institutions emerged. Ancient Greece and Rome saw the rise of moneylenders and rudimentary banks that provided loans and accepted deposits.

The fall of the Roman Empire led to the decline of formal banking in Europe, but the concept thrived elsewhere. During the Middle Ages, Islamic merchants and Jewish traders played a crucial role in reviving and advancing banking practices. Islamic finance, with its principles of profit-sharing and ethical investing, laid the groundwork for modern financial systems.

The Renaissance period marked a resurgence of banking in Europe. Italian city-states like Venice, Florence, and Genoa became financial hubs, thanks to the innovations of banking families such as the Medicis. These bankers developed sophisticated methods for transferring funds, extending credit, and managing risk, laying the foundation for modern banking.

The 17th and 18th centuries saw the establishment of the first modern financial institutions. The Bank of England, founded in 1694, is often considered the prototype of the modern central bank. It was created to manage government debt and issue banknotes, which soon became a widely accepted medium of exchange.

This period also witnessed the rise of stock exchanges, which facilitated the buying and selling of shares in companies. The Amsterdam Stock Exchange, established in 1602, is considered the world's first official stock exchange. It allowed investors to trade shares of the Dutch East India Company, spreading the risk and rewards of exploration and trade ventures.

The Industrial Revolution brought about significant changes in finance. The rapid growth of industries and the need for large-scale investment led to the expansion of capital markets. Banks and financial institutions began offering more sophisticated services, including underwriting, brokerage, and investment banking.

The 19th and early 20th centuries saw further developments in finance. The establishment of the Federal Reserve System in the United States in 1913 aimed to stabilize the banking system and manage monetary policy. This period also witnessed the growth of international finance, with capital flowing across borders to fuel industrial expansion and infrastructure projects.

The Great Depression of the 1930s highlighted the vulnerabilities of the financial system. The stock market crash of 1929 led to widespread bank failures and economic hardship. In response, governments around the world implemented regulatory measures to stabilize the financial system and protect consumers. In the United States, the Glass-Steagall Act separated commercial and investment banking, while the Securities Exchange Act established the Securities and Exchange Commission (SEC) to oversee financial markets.

The post-World War II era brought about unprecedented economic growth and financial innovation. The Bretton Woods Agreement of 1944 established a new international monetary system, pegging currencies to the US dollar and creating the International Monetary Fund (IMF) and the World Bank to promote global economic stability and development.

The latter half of the 20th century saw the rise of electronic banking and the advent of computers in finance. The introduction of credit cards in the 1950s revolutionized consumer spending, while automated teller machines (ATMs) made banking more convenient. The development of electronic funds transfer systems in the 1970s further streamlined financial transactions.

The early 21st century was marked by significant financial upheaval. The dot-com bubble burst in 2000, leading to a recession and highlighting the risks of speculative investment. The global financial crisis of 2008, triggered by the collapse of the housing market and the failure of major financial institutions, had far-reaching consequences. Governments and central banks around the world intervened to stabilize the financial system and prevent a deeper economic collapse.

In response to the crisis, regulatory reforms were implemented to increase transparency, reduce systemic risk, and protect consumers. The Dodd-Frank Wall Street Reform and Consumer Protection Act in the United States aimed to address the root causes of the crisis and strengthen financial oversight.

The past decade has seen the rapid rise of fintech, or financial technology, which has brought about a new wave of innovation in finance. Fintech companies leverage technology to offer a wide range of financial services, from digital payments and peer-to-peer lending to robo-advisors and blockchain-based solutions.

Blockchain technology, the underlying technology behind cryptocurrencies like Bitcoin, has garnered significant attention for its potential to revolutionize finance. By enabling secure, transparent, and decentralized transactions, blockchain has the potential to disrupt traditional financial intermediaries and create new opportunities for innovation.

Artificial intelligence (AI) and machine learning are also transforming finance. These technologies enable financial institutions to analyze vast amounts of data, automate processes, and provide personalized services to customers. AI-powered algorithms are being used for everything from fraud detection and credit scoring to algorithmic trading and investment management.

Mobile banking has become ubiquitous, allowing people to manage their finances from their smartphones. This accessibility has increased financial inclusion, particularly in developing countries where traditional banking infrastructure is lacking. Mobile money platforms like M-Pesa in Kenya have enabled millions of people to access financial services for the first time.

The digital age has also seen the rise of new investment opportunities, such as crowdfunding and initial coin offerings (ICOs). These platforms allow individuals to invest in startups and projects directly, bypassing traditional financial intermediaries. While these innovations have democratized access to investment, they have also introduced new risks and regulatory challenges.

As we look to the future, the financial industry will continue to evolve. The integration of fintech, blockchain, AI, and other emerging technologies will drive further innovation and reshape the way we interact with money. However, this transformation also brings challenges, including the need for robust cybersecurity measures, regulatory oversight, and ethical considerations.

The financial industry has come a long way from its humble beginnings in barter and commodity money. Each stage of its evolution has been marked by innovation, adaptation, and growth. As technology continues to advance, the possibilities for the future of finance are boundless. By understanding this history, we can better appreciate the present and prepare for the opportunities and challenges that lie ahead.

The advent of the digital era has not only changed the tools we use but also the speed and efficiency of financial transactions. High-frequency trading (HFT), for instance, has revolutionized stock trading. HFT uses powerful computers to execute orders at extremely high speeds, allowing traders to capitalize on minute price differences. This practice has significantly increased the volume of trades and the liquidity of markets, though it has also introduced new risks and ethical concerns.

Cryptocurrencies rely on blockchain technology, which is essentially a distributed ledger that records all transactions across a network of computers. This technology ensures transparency and security, as each transaction is verified by network participants through a consensus mechanism. The potential applications of blockchain extend beyond finance to areas like supply chain management, voting systems, and digital identity verification.

Despite their potential, cryptocurrencies face significant challenges. Their volatile nature makes them risky investments, and their association with illicit activities has led to regulatory scrutiny. Governments around the world are grappling with how to regulate these digital assets while fostering innovation.

Another groundbreaking development in finance is the rise of peer-to-peer (P2P) lending platforms. These platforms connect borrowers directly with lenders, bypassing traditional financial institutions. P2P lending has democratized access to credit, allowing individuals and small businesses to obtain loans that might otherwise be unavailable. However, it also presents risks, including the potential for higher default rates and less regulatory protection for investors.

Robo-advisors represent another significant innovation in personal finance. These automated platforms use algorithms to provide financial advice and manage investment portfolios, often at a lower cost than traditional human advisors. Robo-advisors analyze data on market conditions and individual preferences to make investment decisions, offering a level of personalization and efficiency that was previously unattainable.

The integration of AI and machine learning in finance has far-reaching implications. For instance, AI-powered chatbots are being used by banks to provide customer service, answer queries, and even assist with financial planning. These chatbots can handle a large volume of interactions simultaneously, improving efficiency and customer satisfaction.

Machine learning algorithms are also being used to detect fraudulent transactions. By analyzing patterns in transaction data, these algorithms can identify suspicious activities in real-time, reducing the risk of fraud. Additionally, AI is enhancing credit scoring models, allowing lenders to make more accurate assessments of borrowers' creditworthiness.

The digital transformation of finance has not only affected financial institutions but also consumers. Mobile banking apps have become an integral part of daily life, allowing users to check account balances, transfer money, pay bills, and even apply for loans from their smartphones. The convenience and accessibility of mobile banking have made it particularly popular among younger generations.

Financial inclusion has been one of the most significant benefits of digital finance. In developing countries, where traditional banking infrastructure is often lacking, mobile money services have provided millions of people with access to financial services. These services have enabled users to save money, receive payments, and conduct transactions, contributing to economic development and poverty reduction.

The rise of digital finance has also led to the emergence of new regulatory challenges. Ensuring the security and privacy of financial data has become a top priority for regulators and financial institutions. Cybersecurity threats, such as hacking and data breaches, pose significant risks to the stability and integrity of the financial system.

Regulators are also grappling with how to oversee new financial technologies while promoting innovation. The rapid pace of technological change has often outstripped the ability of regulatory frameworks to keep up, leading to calls for more flexible and adaptive regulatory approaches. Balancing the need for consumer protection with the desire to foster innovation is a delicate task that requires ongoing collaboration between regulators, financial institutions, and technology companies.

The evolution of finance has also been shaped by major economic events and crises. The Great Depression of the 1930s, for example, led to significant regulatory changes aimed at stabilizing the financial system and preventing future crises. The introduction of deposit insurance, for instance, helped restore public confidence in the banking system by protecting depositors' funds in the event of a bank failure.

The global financial crisis of 2008 had a profound impact on the financial industry, leading to a wave of regulatory reforms. The crisis exposed significant weaknesses in the financial system, including excessive risk-taking, inadequate oversight, and a lack of transparency. In response, governments and regulators implemented measures to enhance financial stability, increase transparency, and protect consumers.

One of the key lessons from these crises is the importance of effective risk management. Financial institutions have developed sophisticated risk management frameworks to identify, assess, and mitigate various types of risks, including credit, market, operational, and liquidity risks. These frameworks are essential for maintaining the stability and resilience of the financial system.

The role of central banks in managing monetary policy and ensuring financial stability has also evolved. Central banks, such as the Federal Reserve in the United States and the European Central Bank, play a crucial role in regulating the money supply, setting interest rates, and overseeing the banking system. Their actions have a significant impact on economic growth, inflation, and employment.

The globalization of finance has created new opportunities and challenges. The integration of global financial markets has facilitated the flow of capital across borders, enabling businesses to access funding from a diverse pool of investors. However, it has also increased the interconnectedness of financial systems, making them more susceptible to global shocks.

For example, the Asian financial crisis of 1997 and the European sovereign debt crisis of 2010 demonstrated how financial turmoil in one region can quickly spread to others. These crises highlighted the need for international cooperation and coordination to address global financial stability issues. Institutions like the International Monetary Fund (IMF) and the Financial Stability Board (FSB) play a vital role in monitoring and addressing systemic risks in the global financial system.

Financial innovation has been a constant driver of change in the industry. From the development of new financial instruments and products to the creation of novel business models and delivery channels, innovation has continually reshaped the landscape of finance. Innovations such as exchange-traded funds (ETFs), mortgage-backed securities, and credit default swaps have provided investors with new ways to diversify their portfolios and manage risk.

The rise of fintech startups has brought a wave of innovation to the financial industry. These companies leverage technology to create new financial products and services, often targeting underserved segments of the market. For example, microfinance institutions provide small loans to individuals and businesses that lack access to traditional banking services. Similarly, insurtech companies are using technology to offer more affordable and accessible insurance products.

The future of finance will be shaped by several key trends and developments.

One of the most significant trends is the increasing use of data analytics and big data in financial decision-making. Financial institutions are harnessing the power of data to gain insights into customer behavior, optimize operations, and develop personalized financial products.

The adoption of digital currencies, including central bank digital currencies (CBDCs), is another major trend. Several countries, including China and Sweden, are exploring the development of CBDCs to complement their existing monetary systems. These digital currencies have the potential to enhance the efficiency of payments, reduce costs, and improve financial inclusion.

The rise of decentralized finance (DeFi) is also transforming the financial landscape. DeFi leverages blockchain technology to create open and permissionless financial systems that operate without intermediaries. DeFi platforms offer a range of financial services, including lending, borrowing, trading, and asset management, using smart contracts that execute automatically when predefined conditions are met.

Quantum computing represents another frontier in financial innovation. Quantum computers have the potential to solve complex problems much faster than classical computers, opening up new possibilities for financial modeling, risk management, and cryptography. However, the development and practical application of quantum computing in finance are still in their early stages.

The future of finance will also be influenced by ongoing regulatory and ethical considerations. As financial technologies evolve, regulators will need to adapt to ensure that they continue to protect consumers, maintain market integrity, and promote financial stability. Ethical considerations, such as data privacy, algorithmic bias, and the environmental impact of financial activities, will also play a critical role in shaping the future of finance.

In conclusion, the evolution of finance is a story of continuous innovation, adaptation, and growth. From the earliest forms of money and banking to the digital financial systems of today, each stage of this evolution has brought new opportunities and challenges. As we look to the future, the integration of fintech, blockchain, AI, and other emerging technologies will drive further transformation, creating a financial landscape that is more accessible, efficient, and inclusive. By understanding the history and current trends in finance, we can better navigate the opportunities and challenges that lie ahead, and contribute to shaping a more prosperous and equitable financial future.

3

Fintech

Fintech, short for financial technology, is a term that encompasses a wide range of technological innovations in the financial sector. From mobile banking and payment systems to robo-advisors and blockchain technology, fintech has revolutionized how we interact with money and financial services. Understanding fintech is crucial for young people as it impacts everyday financial activities and opens up numerous opportunities for innovation and career development.

Fintech has its roots in the development of digital payment systems, which marked the beginning of a new era in financial services. The proliferation of the internet and smartphones paved the way for platforms like PayPal, Venmo, and Apple Pay, which enable users to make payments quickly and easily without the need for cash or physical credit cards. These platforms have transformed the way we conduct transactions, making it possible to send and receive money with just a few taps on a smartphone. The convenience and speed of digital payments have made them popular worldwide, driving the growth of e-commerce and changing consumer behavior.

One of the most significant aspects of fintech is the rise of peer-to-peer (P2P) lending platforms. Companies like LendingClub and Prosper connect borrowers directly with individual lenders, bypassing traditional financial intermediaries like banks. This model allows borrowers to access loans more easily and often at lower interest rates while enabling lenders to earn higher returns on their investments. P2P lending has democratized access to credit, making it possible for individuals and small businesses to obtain loans that might otherwise be unavailable. This innovation has had a profound impact on the financial industry, challenging traditional banking models and fostering financial inclusion.

Robo-advisors represent another major innovation in personal finance. These automated platforms use algorithms to provide financial advice and manage investment portfolios, often at a lower cost than traditional human advisors. Robo-advisors analyze data on market conditions and individual preferences to make investment decisions, offering a level of personalization and efficiency that was previously unattainable. Companies like Betterment, Wealthfront, and Vanguard's Personal Advisor Services have popularized robo-advisors, making it easier for people to invest and manage their money. By lowering the barriers to entry for investing, robo-advisors have empowered more people to take control of their financial futures.

Blockchain technology, the underlying technology behind cryptocurrencies like Bitcoin, has garnered significant attention for its potential to revolutionize finance. By enabling secure, transparent, and decentralized transactions, blockchain has the potential to disrupt traditional financial intermediaries and create new opportunities for innovation. Blockchain can be used for a wide range of applications beyond cryptocurrencies, including supply chain management, digital identity verification, and smart contracts. The decentralized nature of blockchain means that transactions are verified and recorded by a network of computers, reducing the need for a central authority and increasing security and transparency.

The impact of fintech on the financial industry is profound, bringing both opportunities and challenges. One of the key benefits of fintech is increased financial inclusion. By leveraging technology, fintech companies can reach underserved populations who lack access to traditional banking services. Mobile money platforms, such as M-Pesa in Kenya, have enabled millions of people to access financial services for the first time, allowing them to save money, receive payments, and conduct transactions. This has had a significant positive impact on economic development and poverty reduction in many developing countries. Fintech has the potential to bridge the gap between the unbanked and formal financial services, fostering greater economic participation and growth.

Fintech has also enhanced the efficiency and convenience of financial services. Digital platforms allow users to conduct transactions, manage their finances, and access financial products and services anytime and anywhere. This convenience has made financial services more accessible and user-friendly, particularly for younger generations who are accustomed to digital technology. The ability to check account balances, transfer money, and pay bills from a smartphone has transformed how we manage our finances, making it easier and more convenient to stay on top of our financial obligations.

Big data and analytics play a crucial role in fintech. Financial institutions and fintech companies are harnessing the power of data to gain insights into customer behavior, optimize operations, and develop personalized financial products. For example, data analytics can be used to assess credit risk more accurately, detect fraudulent transactions in real-time, and tailor investment advice to individual preferences. By leveraging data, fintech companies can offer more targeted and effective services, improving customer satisfaction and driving business growth.

Despite its many benefits, fintech also presents challenges and risks. One of the main concerns is cybersecurity. As financial services become increasingly digital, they become more vulnerable to cyberattacks and data breaches. Ensuring the security and privacy of financial data is a top priority for fintech companies and regulators. Robust cybersecurity measures, including encryption, multi-factor authentication, and continuous monitoring, are essential to protect against cyber threats. Companies must invest in advanced security technologies and protocols to safeguard customer information and maintain trust.

Regulatory challenges are another significant hurdle for fintech companies. The rapid pace of technological change often outstrips the ability of regulatory frameworks to keep up. Fintech companies must navigate complex and evolving regulatory landscapes to ensure compliance with laws and regulations. This includes obtaining necessary licenses, adhering to anti-money laundering (AML) and know-your-customer (KYC) requirements, and protecting consumer rights. Balancing the need for regulation with the desire to foster innovation is a delicate task that requires ongoing collaboration between regulators, financial institutions, and technology companies. Effective regulation must ensure that fintech innovations are safe and reliable while promoting competition and innovation.

The integration of fintech into the financial industry has also raised questions about the future of traditional financial institutions. Banks and other established financial institutions face increasing competition from nimble fintech startups that can offer more innovative and cost-effective solutions. To stay competitive, many traditional financial institutions are partnering with fintech companies, investing in fintech startups, or developing their own digital capabilities. This convergence of traditional finance and fintech is driving further innovation and transforming the financial landscape. Established banks are leveraging their resources and customer bases to enhance their digital offerings, while fintech startups bring agility and cutting-edge technology to the table.

The rise of fintech has also influenced the behavior and expectations of consumers. Today's consumers expect seamless, personalized, and real-time financial services. They want to be able to manage their finances on the go, receive instant notifications, and access a wide range of financial products and services through a single digital platform. Fintech companies are meeting these demands by leveraging technology to enhance the customer experience and deliver more value. Personalized financial advice, real-time transaction alerts, and easy access to a variety of financial products have become standard expectations for consumers.

For young people, fintech offers numerous opportunities and advantages. Digital banking apps, investment platforms, and financial planning tools make it easier for young people to manage their money, save for the future, and make informed financial decisions. Fintech also opens up new career opportunities in fields such as data science, software development, cybersecurity, and financial analysis. As the fintech industry continues to grow, the demand for skilled professionals who can develop and manage innovative financial technologies will only increase. Young people with an interest in technology and finance can find exciting and rewarding career paths in the fintech sector.

Fintech is not just transforming personal finance; it is also reshaping the broader financial industry. Payment processing, lending, investment management, insurance, and even regulatory compliance are being revolutionized by fintech innovations. For example, insurtech companies are using technology to streamline the insurance process, offer more personalized policies, and improve claims management. Regtech, or regulatory technology, is helping financial institutions automate compliance processes, monitor transactions for suspicious activity, and ensure adherence to regulatory requirements. These innovations are making financial services more efficient, transparent, and accessible.

The rise of fintech has also influenced the behavior and expectations of consumers. Today's consumers expect seamless, personalized, and real-time financial services. They want to be able to manage their finances on the go, receive instant notifications, and access a wide range of financial products and services through a single digital platform. Fintech companies are meeting these demands by leveraging technology to enhance the customer experience and deliver more value.

As fintech continues to evolve, it will undoubtedly bring about further changes and innovations in the financial industry. Some of the key trends to watch include the increasing use of artificial intelligence and machine learning, the adoption of blockchain and cryptocurrencies, the rise of digital banks, and the development of new payment technologies. These trends will shape the future of finance, offering new opportunities for growth and innovation.

Artificial intelligence (AI) and machine learning are already playing a significant role in fintech. These technologies enable financial institutions to analyze vast amounts of data, automate processes, and provide personalized services to customers. AI-powered algorithms are being used for everything from fraud detection and credit scoring to algorithmic trading and investment management. Machine learning models can identify patterns and trends in data, making it possible to predict customer behavior, optimize pricing, and improve risk management.

Blockchain technology is another major trend in fintech. By enabling secure, transparent, and decentralized transactions, blockchain has the potential to disrupt traditional financial intermediaries and create new opportunities for innovation. Blockchain can be used for a wide range of applications beyond cryptocurrencies, including supply chain management, digital identity verification, and smart contracts. Decentralized finance (DeFi), which leverages blockchain technology to create open and permissionless financial systems, is an emerging area of fintech that is gaining traction.

The rise of digital banks, or neobanks, is another significant development in fintech. Digital banks operate entirely online, without physical branches, and offer a range of banking services through mobile apps and websites. These banks leverage technology to provide a more convenient and user-friendly banking experience, often with lower fees and better interest rates than traditional banks. Examples of digital banks include Chime, N26, and Revolut. The growth of digital banks is changing the competitive landscape of the banking industry, forcing traditional banks to innovate and improve their digital offerings.

Payment technologies are also evolving rapidly. Contactless payments, digital wallets, and biometric authentication are becoming increasingly common, offering consumers more convenient and secure ways to pay. The COVID-19 pandemic has accelerated the adoption of contactless payments, as consumers and businesses seek to minimize physical contact. Digital wallets, such as Apple Pay, Google Pay, and Samsung Pay, allow users to store payment information on their smartphones and make payments with a tap. Biometric authentication, such as fingerprint and facial recognition, adds an extra layer of security to digital payments.

The future of fintech is bright, with endless possibilities for innovation and growth. However, it also comes with challenges and risks. Ensuring the security and privacy of financial data, navigating complex regulatory environments, and addressing ethical concerns will be critical to the success of fintech companies. As technology continues to advance, fintech will play an increasingly important role in shaping the future of finance.

The rapid pace of innovation in fintech is also driving changes in the regulatory landscape. Regulators are working to keep up with new technologies and business models, balancing the need to protect consumers and ensure financial stability with the desire to foster innovation. In some cases, this has led to the development of regulatory sandboxes, which allow fintech companies to test new products and services in a controlled environment before launching them to the broader market. These sandboxes provide a space for experimentation and learning, helping regulators and fintech companies better understand the risks and benefits of new technologies.

Collaboration between fintech companies and traditional financial institutions is also becoming more common. Banks and other established financial institutions are partnering with fintech startups to leverage their technological expertise and innovative solutions. These partnerships can take many forms, from joint ventures and strategic alliances to mergers and acquisitions. By working together, traditional financial institutions and fintech companies can combine their strengths to create more comprehensive and effective financial services.

The global nature of fintech means that developments in one part of the world can have far-reaching implications. For example, the success of mobile money platforms in Africa has inspired similar initiatives in other regions, while regulatory approaches to cryptocurrencies in countries like Japan and Switzerland are being closely watched by regulators elsewhere. As fintech continues to evolve, international cooperation and knowledge sharing will be essential to address common challenges and seize opportunities for innovation.

Financial education is another critical aspect of fintech's impact. As financial services become more digital and complex, it is important for individuals to have a solid understanding of how these services work and how to use them responsibly. Financial literacy programs can help people, especially young people, navigate the fintech landscape and make informed decisions about their money. Schools, community organizations, and fintech companies themselves can play a role in promoting financial education and empowerment.

The potential of fintech to drive social and economic change is immense. By making financial services more accessible and affordable, fintech can help reduce inequality and promote economic inclusion. For example, digital lending platforms can provide microloans to small businesses and entrepreneurs in underserved communities, helping them grow and thrive. Mobile banking can give people in remote areas access to financial services, enabling them to save money, make payments, and participate in the formal economy. These advancements can have a transformative impact on individuals and communities, fostering greater economic participation and development.

The ethical considerations of fintech are also an important area of focus. As financial services become more automated and data-driven, questions about privacy, fairness, and accountability arise. Ensuring that fintech innovations are designed and implemented in a way that respects individuals' rights and promotes social good is essential. This includes addressing issues such as algorithmic bias, data privacy, and the digital divide. By prioritizing ethical considerations, fintech companies can build trust with consumers and create more inclusive and equitable financial systems.

The rise of fintech has also led to the emergence of new business models and revenue streams. For example, subscription-based models are becoming more common in fintech, with companies offering premium services and features for a monthly fee. This can provide a steady stream of revenue and create a more sustainable business model. Other fintech companies generate revenue through transaction fees, interest on loans, and data analytics services. By exploring innovative business models, fintech companies can find new ways to create value and achieve long-term success.

In conclusion, fintech is revolutionizing the financial industry by leveraging technology to deliver innovative financial products and services. From digital payments and P2P lending to robo-advisors and blockchain, fintech is transforming how we save, invest, and manage money. For young people, fintech offers numerous opportunities and advantages, making it easier to manage finances, save for the future, and make informed financial decisions. As fintech continues to evolve, it will undoubtedly bring about further changes and innovations, offering new opportunities for growth and transformation in the financial industry. By understanding the trends and developments in fintech, we can better navigate the opportunities and challenges that lie ahead, and contribute to shaping a more inclusive, efficient, and innovative financial future.

4

Blockchain and Cryptocurrency

Blockchain technology and cryptocurrency have been two of the most transformative innovations in the financial industry over the past decade. They have introduced new ways of thinking about money, transactions, and trust. Understanding blockchain and cryptocurrency is essential for grasping the future of finance and the potential changes it may bring to various aspects of our lives.

Blockchain technology is fundamentally a decentralized, digital ledger that records transactions across multiple computers in such a way that the registered transactions cannot be altered retroactively. This technology was first conceptualized by an individual or group of individuals known as Satoshi Nakamoto, who introduced Bitcoin in 2008. Bitcoin was the first cryptocurrency, and it demonstrated the viability of blockchain technology in maintaining a secure, transparent, and decentralized record of transactions.

The concept of decentralization is central to blockchain technology. Traditional financial systems rely on centralized institutions like banks and governments to verify and record transactions. Blockchain, on the other hand, distributes this responsibility across a network of computers, known as nodes. Each node maintains a copy of the entire blockchain, and transactions are verified through a consensus mechanism. This decentralization makes blockchain more resilient to fraud and tampering, as altering the ledger would require the consensus of the majority of nodes.

Cryptocurrencies, like Bitcoin, operate on blockchain technology. Bitcoin introduced the idea of digital money that is not controlled by any central authority. Instead, it relies on cryptographic principles to secure transactions and control the creation of new units. This has profound implications for the financial industry, as it challenges the traditional roles of banks and governments in managing money and monetary policy.

Since the launch of Bitcoin, thousands of other cryptocurrencies have been created, each with its unique features and applications. Ethereum, for example, introduced the concept of smart contracts—self-executing contracts where the terms of the agreement are written directly into code. Smart contracts run on the Ethereum blockchain and can facilitate, verify, and enforce the performance of contracts without the need for intermediaries. This opens up new possibilities for decentralized applications (DApps) in areas like finance, real estate, and supply chain management.

Cryptocurrencies offer several advantages over traditional currencies and payment systems. They enable fast and low-cost international transfers, provide financial services to the unbanked, and offer an alternative store of value in countries with unstable currencies. However, they also come with challenges and risks. The value of cryptocurrencies can be highly volatile, making them risky investments. Additionally, the anonymity they offer has made them attractive for illegal activities, which has led to increased regulatory scrutiny.

The environmental impact of cryptocurrency mining is another significant concern. Mining, the process by which new cryptocurrency units are created and transactions are verified, requires substantial computational power and energy. Bitcoin mining, in particular, has been criticized for its high energy consumption, which contributes to carbon emissions and environmental degradation. Efforts are being made to develop more energy-efficient mining methods and promote the use of renewable energy sources in mining operations.

The regulatory landscape for cryptocurrencies varies widely across the globe. Some countries, like Japan and Switzerland, have embraced cryptocurrencies and established clear regulatory frameworks to support their growth. Others, like China and India, have taken a more cautious approach, implementing strict regulations or outright bans on cryptocurrency activities. In the United States, regulatory agencies like the Securities and Exchange Commission (SEC) and the Commodity Futures Trading Commission (CFTC) are actively working to develop guidelines for the cryptocurrency market to ensure investor protection and market integrity.

The potential applications of blockchain technology extend far beyond cryptocurrencies. One of the most promising areas is supply chain management. Blockchain can provide a transparent and immutable record of a product's journey from its origin to the consumer, improving traceability, reducing fraud, and increasing efficiency. Companies like IBM and Walmart are already using blockchain to track food products, ensuring food safety and quality.

Another application is digital identity verification. Blockchain can create a secure and tamper-proof digital identity that individuals can use to access various services. This could streamline processes like opening bank accounts, applying for loans, and even voting, while reducing the risk of identity theft and fraud.

Blockchain technology also holds potential in the realm of decentralized finance (DeFi). DeFi leverages blockchain and smart contracts to create financial systems that operate without traditional intermediaries like banks. DeFi platforms offer services such as lending, borrowing, trading, and insurance, all executed through smart contracts on the blockchain. This can make financial services more accessible, transparent, and efficient, but it also introduces new risks, such as smart contract vulnerabilities and regulatory uncertainties.

While blockchain and cryptocurrency offer exciting possibilities, they also present challenges that need to be addressed. Ensuring the security of blockchain networks and protecting against cyber attacks is critical. As blockchain technology becomes more widespread, the importance of developing robust security measures and best practices will grow.

The scalability of blockchain networks is another challenge. As the number of users and transactions increases, so does the demand on the network's capacity. This can lead to slower transaction times and higher fees. Solutions like the Lightning Network for Bitcoin and Ethereum's transition to a proof-of-stake consensus mechanism aim to address these scalability issues, but they are still in development and implementation stages.

The integration of blockchain with other emerging technologies, such as the Internet of Things (IoT) and artificial intelligence (AI), could unlock even more innovative applications. For example, IoT devices could use blockchain to securely share data and automate processes through smart contracts. AI could analyze blockchain data to provide insights and optimize operations. The convergence of these technologies could drive further advancements and create new opportunities across various industries.

For young people, understanding blockchain and cryptocurrency is crucial as these technologies are likely to play a significant role in the future of finance and beyond. Learning about how blockchain works, the principles of decentralization, and the potential applications of smart contracts can provide valuable knowledge and skills. Additionally, gaining insights into the regulatory and ethical considerations surrounding these technologies will be important for navigating the evolving landscape.

The rise of blockchain and cryptocurrency has also created new career opportunities. From blockchain developers and cryptographers to compliance officers and legal experts, the demand for professionals with expertise in these areas is growing. Young people with a strong foundation in computer science, cryptography, and financial regulations will be well-positioned to pursue careers in this dynamic and rapidly evolving field.

In conclusion, blockchain technology and cryptocurrency have introduced groundbreaking innovations that are transforming the financial industry and beyond. By enabling secure, transparent, and decentralized transactions, these technologies offer numerous benefits, including increased financial inclusion, enhanced efficiency, and new opportunities for innovation. However, they also present challenges and risks that need to be addressed, such as cybersecurity, regulatory compliance, and environmental impact.

As blockchain and cryptocurrency continue to evolve, they will likely play an increasingly important role in shaping the future of finance and various other sectors. Understanding these technologies and their implications will be essential for navigating the opportunities and challenges that lie ahead. For young people, gaining knowledge and skills in blockchain and cryptocurrency can open up exciting career prospects and contribute to the development of a more inclusive, efficient, and innovative financial system.

The potential of blockchain technology to disrupt and innovate extends to numerous other areas beyond finance. In healthcare, for example, blockchain can be used to securely store and share patient records, ensuring privacy and improving the coordination of care. In real estate, blockchain can streamline property transactions by providing a transparent and tamper-proof record of ownership and transfer. In supply chains, blockchain can enhance traceability and reduce fraud by providing a clear record of a product's journey from origin to consumer.

The concept of tokenization, enabled by blockchain technology, is another emerging trend. Tokenization involves converting physical or digital assets into digital tokens that can be traded on a blockchain. This can include anything from real estate and art to stocks and bonds. Tokenization can increase liquidity, reduce transaction costs, and make it easier to trade and invest in assets. It also opens up new possibilities for fractional ownership, allowing individuals to invest in a portion of an asset rather than the whole, which can lower barriers to entry and democratize access to investment opportunities.

The rise of non-fungible tokens (NFTs) is a notable example of tokenization. NFTs are unique digital tokens that represent ownership of a specific item, such as digital art, collectibles, or virtual real estate. Unlike cryptocurrencies like Bitcoin, which are fungible and interchangeable, each NFT is distinct and cannot be replaced by another. NFTs have gained significant attention and popularity, with high-profile sales and growing interest from artists, creators, and investors. They offer a new way to buy, sell, and trade digital assets, but also raise questions about intellectual property, copyright, and the environmental impact of blockchain.

The environmental impact of blockchain and cryptocurrency is a critical issue that needs to be addressed. Bitcoin mining, in particular, requires significant computational power and energy, leading to concerns about its carbon footprint. Efforts are being made to develop more energy-efficient consensus mechanisms, such as proof-of-stake, which is being implemented by Ethereum. Additionally, the use of renewable energy sources for mining operations can help mitigate the environmental impact. As the adoption of blockchain and cryptocurrency grows, it will be important to prioritize sustainability and develop solutions that balance innovation with environmental responsibility.

Regulation is another key factor in the future of blockchain and cryptocurrency. Governments and regulatory bodies are grappling with how to oversee these technologies and ensure they are used responsibly. Clear and consistent regulatory frameworks can provide stability and protect consumers while fostering innovation. International cooperation and coordination will be essential to address cross-border issues and create a cohesive regulatory environment. The role of self-regulatory organizations (SROs) and industry standards will also be important in promoting best practices and ethical behavior.

The integration of blockchain with other emerging technologies, such as the Internet of Things (IoT) and artificial intelligence (AI), holds great promise. For example, IoT devices can use blockchain to securely share data and automate processes through smart contracts. This can enable new applications in areas like supply chain management, smart cities, and autonomous vehicles. AI can analyze blockchain data to provide insights, optimize operations, and improve decision-making. The convergence of these technologies can drive further advancements and create new opportunities across various industries.

Education and awareness will play a crucial role in the adoption and development of blockchain and cryptocurrency. As these technologies become more prevalent, it is important for individuals to understand how they work and how to use them safely and responsibly. Financial literacy programs, educational initiatives, and public awareness campaigns can help demystify blockchain and cryptocurrency and empower people to make informed decisions. Schools, universities, and online platforms can offer courses and resources to teach the fundamentals of blockchain, cryptography, and decentralized finance.

In summary, blockchain technology and cryptocurrency have introduced groundbreaking innovations that are transforming the financial industry and beyond. By enabling secure, transparent, and decentralized transactions, these technologies offer numerous benefits, including increased financial inclusion, enhanced efficiency, and new opportunities for innovation. However, they also present challenges and risks that need to be addressed, such as cybersecurity, regulatory compliance, and environmental impact.

As blockchain and cryptocurrency continue to evolve, they will likely play an increasingly important role in shaping the future of finance and various other sectors. Understanding these technologies and their implications will be essential for navigating the opportunities and challenges that lie ahead. For young people, gaining knowledge and skills in blockchain and cryptocurrency can open up exciting career prospects and contribute to the development of a more inclusive, efficient, and innovative financial system.

The potential applications of blockchain technology are vast and varied, spanning multiple industries and use cases. From supply chain management and digital identity verification to healthcare and real estate, blockchain can enhance transparency, security, and efficiency. The concept of tokenization, including the rise of non-fungible tokens (NFTs), is transforming how we buy, sell, and trade assets, offering new opportunities for investment and ownership.

Addressing the environmental impact of blockchain and cryptocurrency is critical to ensuring their sustainability. Efforts to develop more energy-efficient consensus mechanisms and use renewable energy sources can help mitigate the environmental footprint. Regulation will play a key role in shaping the future of these technologies, providing stability and protection while fostering innovation. International cooperation and self-regulatory organizations will be essential in creating a cohesive regulatory environment.

The integration of blockchain with other emerging technologies, such as IoT and AI, holds great promise for driving further advancements and creating new opportunities. Education and awareness are crucial for the widespread adoption and responsible use of blockchain and cryptocurrency. By understanding these technologies, individuals can make informed decisions and contribute to the development of a more inclusive, efficient, and innovative financial system.

In conclusion, blockchain technology and cryptocurrency represent a paradigm shift in how we think about money, transactions, and trust. Their potential to transform the financial industry and beyond is immense, offering new possibilities for innovation and growth. By addressing the challenges and leveraging the opportunities, we can shape a future where blockchain and cryptocurrency contribute to a more inclusive, transparent, and efficient global economy. For young people, understanding and engaging with these technologies can open up exciting career prospects and empower them to be active participants in the evolving landscape of finance.

5

Artificial Intelligence and Machine Learning

Artificial Intelligence (AI) and Machine Learning (ML) are rapidly transforming the financial industry. These technologies are revolutionizing how financial institutions operate, how they interact with customers, and how financial decisions are made. Understanding AI and ML is crucial for grasping the future of finance and the potential changes these technologies may bring to various aspects of the industry.

AI refers to the simulation of human intelligence processes by machines, particularly computer systems. These processes include learning (the acquisition of information and rules for using the information), reasoning (using rules to reach approximate or definite conclusions), and self-correction. Machine Learning, a subset of AI, involves the use of algorithms and statistical models to enable computers to improve their performance on a specific task through experience.

In finance, AI and ML are being applied in various ways to enhance efficiency, accuracy, and decision-making. One of the most significant applications of AI in finance is algorithmic trading. Algorithmic trading uses complex AI algorithms to make trading decisions at speeds and frequencies that are impossible for human traders. These algorithms analyze vast amounts of market data, identify patterns, and execute trades based on predefined criteria. This has led to increased market efficiency and liquidity but has also raised concerns about market volatility and the potential for flash crashes.

AI is also transforming the way financial institutions manage risk. Risk management is a critical function in finance, and AI algorithms can analyze large datasets to identify potential risks and predict future trends. For example, AI can be used to assess credit risk by analyzing a borrower's credit history, transaction patterns, and other relevant data points. This allows lenders to make more informed decisions and reduce the likelihood of defaults.

Fraud detection is another area where AI is making a significant impact. Financial fraud is a major concern for banks and other financial institutions, and traditional methods of fraud detection often struggle to keep up with the sophisticated techniques used by fraudsters. AI and ML algorithms can analyze transaction data in real-time, identify unusual patterns, and flag potentially fraudulent activities. This enables financial institutions to respond quickly and prevent significant losses.

Customer service is also being transformed by AI through the use of chatbots and virtual assistants. These AI-powered tools can handle a wide range of customer inquiries, from answering basic questions to assisting with complex transactions. By automating routine tasks, chatbots free up human agents to focus on more complex issues, improving overall customer satisfaction. Additionally, AI can analyze customer data to provide personalized financial advice and recommendations, enhancing the customer experience.

Another important application of AI in finance is in portfolio management and investment. Robo-advisors, which use AI algorithms to provide investment advice and manage portfolios, are becoming increasingly popular. These platforms analyze market data and individual investor preferences to create and manage investment portfolios. Robo-advisors offer several advantages, including lower fees, accessibility, and personalized investment strategies, making them an attractive option for a wide range of investors.

AI and ML are also being used to improve regulatory compliance. Financial institutions are subject to a myriad of regulations, and ensuring compliance can be a complex and time-consuming process. AI can streamline compliance by automating tasks such as monitoring transactions for suspicious activity, ensuring adherence to anti-money laundering (AML) and know-your-customer (KYC) regulations, and generating compliance reports. This not only reduces the burden on compliance teams but also helps financial institutions stay ahead of regulatory changes.

Despite the many benefits of AI and ML, their adoption in finance also raises several ethical and practical concerns. One of the primary concerns is the potential for bias in AI algorithms. Since AI systems learn from historical data, they can inadvertently perpetuate existing biases present in the data. For example, an AI algorithm used for credit scoring might discriminate against certain demographic groups if the training data reflects historical biases. Ensuring fairness and transparency in AI systems is crucial to prevent such issues.

Another concern is the potential loss of jobs due to automation. As AI and ML systems take over tasks previously performed by humans, there is a fear that many jobs in the financial industry may become obsolete. While automation can lead to increased efficiency and cost savings, it is important to consider the social implications and ensure that workers are provided with opportunities for retraining and reskilling.

The reliance on AI also raises questions about accountability and decision-making. If an AI algorithm makes a mistake or a decision leads to negative consequences, it can be challenging to determine who is responsible. Establishing clear guidelines and accountability frameworks is essential to address these issues and ensure that AI systems are used responsibly.

The integration of AI and ML in finance also requires robust data security measures. Financial institutions handle vast amounts of sensitive data, and ensuring the security and privacy of this data is paramount. Cybersecurity threats, such as data breaches and hacking, pose significant risks to the integrity of AI systems. Implementing advanced security protocols and continuously monitoring for vulnerabilities are crucial to protect against these threats.

The future of AI and ML in finance holds immense potential. As these technologies continue to evolve, they will likely bring about further innovations and transformations in the industry. Some of the key trends to watch include the development of more advanced AI algorithms, the integration of AI with other emerging technologies such as blockchain, and the increasing use of AI for predictive analytics and decision-making.

One of the most promising areas of AI research is in the development of explainable AI (XAI). Traditional AI systems, particularly deep learning models, often operate as "black boxes," making it difficult to understand how they arrive at their decisions. XAI aims to create AI systems that are transparent and can provide clear explanations for their decisions. This is particularly important in finance, where understanding the rationale behind investment recommendations, credit approvals, and risk assessments is crucial for regulatory compliance and trust.

The integration of AI with blockchain technology also holds great promise. Blockchain's decentralized and immutable nature can enhance the security and transparency of AI systems, while AI can improve the efficiency and scalability of blockchain networks. For example, AI algorithms can be used to optimize consensus mechanisms in blockchain, enhance fraud detection, and automate smart contract execution. The convergence of these technologies can drive further innovation and create new opportunities in the financial industry.

Predictive analytics is another area where AI is expected to make significant advancements. By analyzing historical data and identifying patterns, AI can provide valuable insights and forecasts for various financial activities, such as market trends, investment opportunities, and risk management. Predictive analytics can help financial institutions make more informed decisions, optimize their strategies, and stay ahead of market developments.

For young people, understanding AI and ML is crucial as these technologies are likely to play a significant role in the future of finance. Learning about the principles of AI, the various applications of ML, and the ethical and practical considerations of these technologies can provide valuable knowledge and skills. Additionally, gaining insights into the regulatory and security aspects of AI and ML will be important for navigating the evolving landscape.

The rise of AI and ML has also created new career opportunities. From data scientists and machine learning engineers to AI ethicists and cybersecurity experts, the demand for professionals with expertise in these areas is growing. Young people with a strong foundation in computer science, data analysis, and financial regulations will be well-positioned to pursue careers in this dynamic and rapidly evolving field.

In conclusion, AI and ML are transforming the financial industry by enhancing efficiency, accuracy, and decision-making. These technologies offer numerous benefits, including improved risk management, fraud detection, customer service, and investment strategies. However, their adoption also raises ethical and practical concerns, such as bias, job displacement, accountability, and data security.

As AI and ML continue to evolve, they will likely bring about further innovations and transformations in the financial industry. Understanding these technologies and their implications will be essential for navigating the opportunities and challenges that lie ahead. For young people, gaining knowledge and skills in AI and ML can open up exciting career prospects and contribute to the development of a more efficient, transparent, and innovative financial system.

The potential applications of AI and ML extend far beyond finance, spanning various industries and use cases. From healthcare and education to transportation and entertainment, these technologies are driving advancements and creating new possibilities. By addressing the challenges and leveraging the opportunities, we can shape a future where AI and ML contribute to a more inclusive, efficient, and sustainable global economy.

Education and awareness will play a crucial role in the adoption and development of AI and ML. As these technologies become more prevalent, it is important for individuals to understand how they work and how to use them responsibly. Financial literacy programs, educational initiatives, and public awareness campaigns can help demystify AI and ML and empower people to make informed decisions. Schools, universities, and online platforms can offer courses and resources to teach the fundamentals of AI, machine learning, and data science.

The ethical considerations of AI and ML are also an important area of focus. As financial services become more automated and data-driven, questions about privacy, fairness, and accountability arise. Ensuring that AI innovations are designed and implemented in a way that respects individuals' rights and promotes social good is essential. This includes addressing issues such as algorithmic bias, data privacy, and the digital divide. By prioritizing ethical considerations, fintech companies can build trust with consumers and create more inclusive and equitable financial systems.

The rise of AI and ML has also led to the emergence of new business models and revenue streams. For example, subscription-based models are becoming more common in fintech, with companies offering premium services and features for a monthly fee. This can provide a steady stream of revenue and create a more sustainable business model. Other fintech companies generate revenue through transaction fees, interest on loans, and data analytics services. By exploring innovative business models, fintech companies can find new ways to create value and achieve long-term success.

In conclusion, AI and ML represent a paradigm shift in how we think about finance and decision-making. Their potential to transform the financial industry and beyond is immense, offering new possibilities for innovation and growth. By addressing the challenges and leveraging the opportunities, we can shape a future where AI and ML contribute to a more inclusive, transparent, and efficient global economy. For young people, understanding and engaging with these technologies can open up exciting career prospects and empower them to be active participants in the evolving landscape of finance.

6

Mobile Banking

Mobile banking has emerged as one of the most significant innovations in the financial sector, revolutionizing the way people interact with their finances. This chapter explores the evolution of mobile banking, its benefits and drawbacks, its impact on financial inclusion, and the future trends shaping this dynamic field.

Mobile banking refers to the use of smartphones and other mobile devices to access banking services and perform financial transactions. This technology allows users to check account balances, transfer funds, pay bills, deposit checks, and even apply for loans without needing to visit a physical bank branch. The convenience and accessibility of mobile banking have made it increasingly popular, particularly among younger generations who are more comfortable with digital technology.

The origins of mobile banking can be traced back to the early 2000s when banks began offering basic SMS-based services. Customers could check their account balances and receive transaction alerts via text messages. However, the true revolution in mobile banking began with the advent of smartphones and the development of mobile banking apps. These apps provided a user-friendly interface and a wide range of functionalities, making it easier for customers to manage their finances on the go.

One of the most significant benefits of mobile banking is its convenience. Users can perform banking transactions anytime and anywhere, eliminating the need to visit a bank branch during working hours. This convenience is particularly valuable for individuals with busy schedules, those living in remote areas, or people with limited mobility. Mobile banking also offers real-time access to account information, enabling users to monitor their finances closely and make informed decisions.

Another major advantage of mobile banking is its ability to enhance financial inclusion. In many developing countries, traditional banking infrastructure is lacking, and large segments of the population remain unbanked. Mobile banking provides an accessible and affordable way for these individuals to access financial services. For example, mobile money platforms like M-Pesa in Kenya have enabled millions of people to perform transactions, save money, and receive payments using their mobile phones. This has had a significant positive impact on economic development and poverty reduction.

Mobile banking also promotes financial literacy by providing users with easy access to financial information and tools. Many mobile banking apps offer features such as budgeting tools, spending trackers, and financial education resources. These tools can help users better understand their financial situation, develop good financial habits, and make smarter financial decisions. By empowering individuals with knowledge and tools, mobile banking can contribute to greater financial stability and well-being.

Despite its many benefits, mobile banking also presents several challenges and risks. One of the primary concerns is security. Mobile banking involves the transmission of sensitive financial information over the internet, making it a target for cybercriminals. Phishing attacks, malware, and fraudulent apps are common threats that can compromise the security of mobile banking transactions. To mitigate these risks, banks and app developers must implement robust security measures, such as encryption, multi-factor authentication, and regular security updates.

Another challenge is the digital divide. While mobile banking has the potential to enhance financial inclusion, it also requires access to mobile devices and reliable internet connectivity. In regions where these resources are scarce, the adoption of mobile banking may be limited. Efforts to expand access to affordable mobile devices and internet services are crucial to ensuring that the benefits of mobile banking are accessible to all.

User experience is another critical factor in the success of mobile banking. A poorly designed app with a complicated interface can frustrate users and discourage them from using mobile banking services. Banks must invest in user-friendly design and continuous improvements to provide a seamless and intuitive experience. Features such as easy navigation, clear instructions, and responsive customer support can significantly enhance the usability of mobile banking apps.

The future of mobile banking is likely to be shaped by several emerging trends and technologies. One of the most promising trends is the integration of artificial intelligence (AI) and machine learning (ML) into mobile banking apps. AI-powered chatbots and virtual assistants can provide personalized customer support, answer queries, and even offer financial advice. Machine learning algorithms can analyze transaction data to detect fraudulent activities, predict customer needs, and provide tailored financial solutions.

Another significant trend is the adoption of biometric authentication methods. Fingerprint recognition, facial recognition, and voice recognition can provide a higher level of security and convenience compared to traditional passwords. Biometric authentication can reduce the risk of unauthorized access and make it easier for users to log in to their mobile banking apps.

The rise of open banking is also likely to influence the future of mobile banking. Open banking involves the sharing of financial data between banks and third-party service providers through secure APIs (Application Programming Interfaces). This can enable the development of innovative financial services and apps that provide greater value to customers. For example, third-party apps can aggregate information from multiple bank accounts, provide personalized financial insights, and offer tailored financial products.

The use of blockchain technology in mobile banking is another area to watch. Blockchain can enhance the security and transparency of financial transactions, reduce the risk of fraud, and streamline cross-border payments. Some banks are already exploring the use of blockchain for various applications, and its integration into mobile banking could bring significant benefits.

Mobile banking is also likely to play a crucial role in the rise of digital currencies. Central banks around the world are exploring the development of central bank digital currencies (CBDCs), which could be integrated into mobile banking platforms. Digital currencies can provide a more efficient and secure means of payment, reduce transaction costs, and enhance financial inclusion.

The impact of mobile banking on traditional banking is profound. As more customers shift to digital channels, the demand for physical bank branches is declining. This has led many banks to re-evaluate their branch networks and invest more in digital transformation. Some banks are closing branches and redirecting resources to enhance their digital capabilities, while others are transforming branches into advisory centers that focus on providing high-value services.

The rise of neobanks, or digital-only banks, is another significant development in the mobile banking landscape. Neobanks operate entirely online, without physical branches, and offer a range of banking services through mobile apps. These banks leverage technology to provide a more convenient, cost-effective, and customer-centric banking experience. Examples of neobanks include Chime, N26, and Revolut. The growth of neobanks is changing the competitive dynamics of the banking industry, forcing traditional banks to innovate and improve their digital offerings.

For young people, mobile banking offers numerous opportunities and advantages. The ability to manage finances on the go, access financial information in real-time, and use digital tools for budgeting and saving can help young people develop good financial habits and achieve their financial goals. Mobile banking also provides a platform for financial education, with many apps offering resources and tools to help users understand and improve their financial health.

In conclusion, mobile banking is transforming the financial industry by making banking services more accessible, convenient, and efficient. The evolution of mobile banking from basic SMS-based services to sophisticated mobile apps has revolutionized how people manage their finances. While mobile banking offers numerous benefits, it also presents challenges and risks that need to be addressed. Security, user experience, and the digital divide are critical factors that must be considered to ensure the success and inclusivity of mobile banking.

The future of mobile banking is bright, with emerging trends and technologies promising to enhance the customer experience and expand the range of services offered. The integration of AI and machine learning, the adoption of biometric authentication, the rise of open banking, the use of blockchain technology, and the development of digital currencies are all set to shape the future of mobile banking.

For young people, understanding and leveraging mobile banking can provide valuable skills and opportunities. As the financial industry continues to evolve, mobile banking will play an increasingly important role in shaping the future of finance. By staying informed about the latest trends and developments, young people can make the most of the opportunities offered by mobile banking and contribute to the development of a more inclusive and innovative financial system.

The Evolution of Mobile Banking

The story of mobile banking begins with the rise of mobile phones in the late 20th century. Initially, mobile phones were used for basic communication, but as technology advanced, they became more versatile and capable of performing a wider range of functions. The introduction of SMS (Short Message Service) allowed banks to offer simple text-based services, such as balance inquiries and transaction alerts. These early services were limited in functionality but marked the beginning of mobile banking.

The real transformation began with the advent of smartphones in the late 2000s. Smartphones, with their advanced computing power, touchscreens, and internet connectivity, opened up new possibilities for mobile banking. Banks started developing mobile apps that provided a more comprehensive and user-friendly banking experience. These apps allowed customers to perform a wide range of transactions, from transferring funds and paying bills to depositing checks and applying for loans.

One of the key factors driving the adoption of mobile banking was the widespread availability of affordable smartphones and mobile data plans. As smartphones became more accessible, a larger segment of the population could take advantage of mobile banking services. The convenience of being able to perform banking transactions anytime and anywhere resonated with users, leading to a rapid increase in the use of mobile banking apps.

The rise of mobile banking also coincided with the growth of the fintech industry. Fintech companies, leveraging the power of technology, developed innovative financial products and services that complemented traditional banking. Mobile banking apps started integrating these fintech solutions, offering features such as peer-to-peer payments, investment management, and personal finance tools. This integration further enhanced the value proposition of mobile banking and attracted more users.

Benefits of Mobile Banking

Mobile banking offers numerous benefits that have contributed to its widespread adoption. One of the most significant advantages is convenience. Users can access their bank accounts and perform transactions from the comfort of their homes, offices, or even while traveling. This eliminates the need to visit a physical bank branch, saving time and effort. The ability to perform transactions 24/7 is particularly valuable in today's fast-paced world, where people often have busy schedules and limited time for banking errands.

Real-time access to account information is another major benefit of mobile banking. Users can check their account balances, view transaction history, and receive instant notifications of account activity. This real-time visibility helps users stay on top of their finances and quickly identify any unauthorized transactions or discrepancies. The ability to monitor account activity in real-time provides peace of mind and enhances financial security.

Mobile banking also offers cost savings for both banks and customers. For banks, mobile banking reduces the need for physical branches and associated operational costs. This allows banks to allocate resources more efficiently and invest in digital infrastructure and innovation. For customers, mobile banking eliminates the need to travel to a bank branch, saving on transportation costs. Additionally, many mobile banking services are offered free of charge or at a lower cost compared to traditional banking services, providing further savings for users.

Enhancing Financial Inclusion

One of the most transformative impacts of mobile banking is its ability to enhance financial inclusion. In many developing countries, traditional banking infrastructure is limited, and a significant portion of the population remains unbanked. Mobile banking provides an accessible and affordable solution for these individuals to access financial services. Mobile money platforms, such as M-Pesa in Kenya, have revolutionized financial inclusion by enabling users to perform transactions, save money, and receive payments using their mobile phones.

The success of mobile money platforms in Africa has inspired similar initiatives in other regions. For example, in India, the government's Digital India initiative and the widespread adoption of mobile phones have led to the rapid growth of mobile banking and digital payments. Mobile banking has also played a crucial role in financial inclusion efforts in Latin America and Southeast Asia, where traditional banking infrastructure is often inadequate.

Mobile banking enables underserved populations to participate in the formal financial system, providing them with opportunities to save money, access credit, and build financial resilience. By offering a convenient and affordable way to access financial services, mobile banking can contribute to economic development and poverty reduction. The ability to perform transactions and save money using a mobile phone can have a transformative impact on individuals' lives, helping them manage their finances more effectively and achieve their financial goals.

Financial Literacy and Empowerment

Mobile banking also promotes financial literacy and empowerment by providing users with easy access to financial information and tools. Many mobile banking apps offer features such as budgeting tools, spending trackers, and financial education resources. These tools can help users better understand their financial situation, develop good financial habits, and make smarter financial decisions.

For example, budgeting tools can help users create and stick to a budget by tracking their income and expenses. Spending trackers can provide insights into spending patterns, helping users identify areas where they can cut costs and save money. Financial education resources, such as articles, videos, and tutorials, can provide valuable information on topics like saving, investing, and managing debt.

By empowering individuals with knowledge and tools, mobile banking can contribute to greater financial stability and well-being. Financial literacy is a critical component of financial health, and mobile banking provides a platform for users to learn and improve their financial skills. This empowerment can have a positive impact on individuals' lives, helping them make informed decisions and achieve their financial goals.

Security and Privacy Concerns

Despite its many benefits, mobile banking also presents several challenges and risks, with security being a primary concern. Mobile banking involves the transmission of sensitive financial information over the internet, making it a target for cybercriminals. Phishing attacks, malware, and fraudulent apps are common threats that can compromise the security of mobile banking transactions.

To mitigate these risks, banks and app developers must implement robust security measures. Encryption is essential to protect data during transmission, ensuring that sensitive information cannot be intercepted and read by unauthorized parties. Multi-factor authentication (MFA) adds an extra layer of security by requiring users to verify their identity using multiple methods, such as a password and a fingerprint scan.

Regular security updates and patches are also crucial to address vulnerabilities and protect against emerging threats. Banks must continuously monitor for suspicious activity and respond quickly to security incidents to minimize the impact on users. Educating customers about safe practices, such as avoiding public Wi-Fi for banking transactions and recognizing phishing attempts, is also important for enhancing security.

Privacy concerns are another significant issue in mobile banking. The collection and storage of personal and financial information by mobile banking apps raise questions about data privacy and protection. Banks must adhere to strict data privacy regulations and implement measures to protect customer information from unauthorized access and misuse. Transparency about data collection practices and giving customers control over their data can help build trust and confidence in mobile banking services.

The Digital Divide

While mobile banking has the potential to enhance financial inclusion, it also requires access to mobile devices and reliable internet connectivity. In regions where these resources are scarce, the adoption of mobile banking may be limited. The digital divide, the gap between those who have access to digital technologies and those who do not, remains a significant challenge.

Efforts to expand access to affordable mobile devices and internet services are crucial to ensuring that the benefits of mobile banking are accessible to all. Governments, non-profit organizations, and private companies can play a role in bridging the digital divide by investing in infrastructure, providing subsidies for mobile devices, and promoting digital literacy programs.

Digital literacy is also an important factor in the adoption of mobile banking. Users need to be comfortable with using mobile devices and navigating digital interfaces to take full advantage of mobile banking services. Digital literacy programs can help individuals develop the skills and confidence needed to use mobile banking apps effectively.

User Experience and Design

User experience (UX) is a critical factor in the success of mobile banking. A well-designed app with an intuitive interface can enhance usability and encourage adoption, while a poorly designed app can frustrate users and discourage them from using mobile banking services.

Banks must invest in user-friendly design and continuous improvements to provide a seamless and intuitive experience. Features such as easy navigation, clear instructions, and responsive customer support can significantly enhance the usability of mobile banking apps. Personalization is also important, as users appreciate apps that cater to their individual needs and preferences.

Usability testing and user feedback are essential for identifying pain points and areas for improvement. By involving users in the design process and making iterative improvements based on feedback, banks can create mobile banking apps that meet the needs and expectations of their customers.

Emerging Trends and Future Directions

The future of mobile banking is likely to be shaped by several emerging trends and technologies. One of the most promising trends is the integration of artificial intelligence (AI) and machine learning (ML) into mobile banking apps. AI-powered chatbots and virtual assistants can provide personalized customer support, answer queries, and even offer financial advice. Machine learning algorithms can analyze transaction data to detect fraudulent activities, predict customer needs, and provide tailored financial solutions.

Another significant trend is the adoption of biometric authentication methods. Fingerprint recognition, facial recognition, and voice recognition can provide a higher level of security and convenience compared to traditional passwords. Biometric authentication can reduce the risk of unauthorized access and make it easier for users to log in to their mobile banking apps.

The rise of open banking is also likely to influence the future of mobile banking. Open banking involves the sharing of financial data between banks and third-party service providers through secure APIs (Application Programming Interfaces). This can enable the development of innovative financial services and apps that provide greater value to customers. For example, third-party apps can aggregate information from multiple bank accounts, provide personalized financial insights, and offer tailored financial products.

The use of blockchain technology in mobile banking is another area to watch. Blockchain can enhance the security and transparency of financial transactions, reduce the risk of fraud, and streamline cross-border payments. Some banks are already exploring the use of blockchain for various applications, and its integration into mobile banking could bring significant benefits.

Mobile banking is also likely to play a crucial role in the rise of digital currencies. Central banks around the world are exploring the development of central bank digital currencies (CBDCs), which could be integrated into mobile banking platforms. Digital currencies can provide a more efficient and secure means of payment, reduce transaction costs, and enhance financial inclusion.

The impact of mobile banking on traditional banking is profound. As more customers shift to digital channels, the demand for physical bank branches is declining. This has led many banks to re-evaluate their branch networks and invest more in digital transformation. Some banks are closing branches and redirecting resources to enhance their digital capabilities, while others are transforming branches into advisory centers that focus on providing high-value services.

The rise of neobanks, or digital-only banks, is another significant development in the mobile banking landscape. Neobanks operate entirely online, without physical branches, and offer a range of banking services through mobile apps. These banks leverage technology to provide a more convenient, cost-effective, and customer-centric banking experience. Examples of neobanks include Chime, N26, and Revolut. The growth of neobanks is changing the competitive dynamics of the banking industry, forcing traditional banks to innovate and improve their digital offerings.

The Role of Mobile Banking in Financial Education

Mobile banking has the potential to play a significant role in financial education. Many mobile banking apps offer features and resources designed to help users improve their financial literacy. These tools can provide valuable insights into spending habits, budgeting, saving, and investing, empowering users to make informed financial decisions.

For example, spending trackers can help users monitor their expenses and identify areas where they can cut costs. Budgeting tools can assist users in creating and sticking to a budget, helping them manage their finances more effectively. Financial education resources, such as articles, videos, and tutorials, can provide information on a wide range of topics, from basic financial concepts to more advanced investment strategies.

By offering these educational resources, mobile banking apps can help users develop good financial habits and achieve their financial goals. Financial literacy is a critical component of financial health, and mobile banking provides a convenient and accessible platform for users to learn and improve their financial skills.

Mobile Banking and the Gig Economy

The rise of the gig economy has also influenced the adoption and development of mobile banking. Gig workers, such as freelancers, independent contractors, and ride-share drivers, often have unique financial needs that differ from those of traditional employees. Mobile banking can provide gig workers with the tools and services they need to manage their finances effectively.

For example, mobile banking apps can offer features such as instant payment options, allowing gig workers to access their earnings immediately after completing a job. Budgeting tools can help gig workers manage irregular income and expenses, while savings features can assist them in setting aside money for taxes, emergencies, and other financial goals.

Some mobile banking apps also offer tailored financial products for gig workers, such as loans and insurance specifically designed to meet their needs. By addressing the unique financial challenges faced by gig workers, mobile banking can support the growth and sustainability of the gig economy.

Challenges and Considerations for the Future

While the future of mobile banking is promising, there are several challenges and considerations that must be addressed to ensure its continued success and inclusivity. Security and privacy concerns remain paramount, as the transmission of sensitive financial information over the internet makes mobile banking a target for cybercriminals. Banks and app developers must continuously invest in advanced security measures and educate users about safe practices.

The digital divide is another significant challenge that needs to be addressed. Expanding access to affordable mobile devices and reliable internet services is crucial to ensuring that the benefits of mobile banking are accessible to all. Digital literacy programs can help individuals develop the skills and confidence needed to use mobile banking apps effectively.

User experience and design are also critical factors in the success of mobile banking. Banks must invest in user-friendly design and continuous improvements to provide a seamless and intuitive experience. Personalization, usability testing, and user feedback are essential for creating mobile banking apps that meet the needs and expectations of customers.

Regulatory considerations are also important. As mobile banking continues to evolve, regulators must ensure that the regulatory framework keeps pace with technological advancements. Clear and consistent regulations can provide stability and protect consumers while fostering innovation. International cooperation and coordination will be essential to address cross-border issues and create a cohesive regulatory environment.

Conclusion

Mobile banking is transforming the financial industry by making banking services more accessible, convenient, and efficient. The evolution of mobile banking from basic SMS-based services to sophisticated mobile apps has revolutionized how people manage their finances. While mobile banking offers numerous benefits, it also presents challenges and risks that need to be addressed. Security, user experience, and the digital divide are critical factors that must be considered to ensure the success and inclusivity of mobile banking.

The future of mobile banking is bright, with emerging trends and technologies promising to enhance the customer experience and expand the range of services offered. The integration of AI and machine learning, the adoption of biometric authentication, the rise of open banking, the use of blockchain technology, and the development of digital currencies are all set to shape the future of mobile banking.

For young people, understanding and leveraging mobile banking can provide valuable skills and opportunities. As the financial industry continues to evolve, mobile banking will play an increasingly important role in shaping the future of finance. By staying informed about the latest trends and developments, young people can make the most of the opportunities offered by mobile banking and contribute to the development of a more inclusive and innovative financial system.

In summary, mobile banking represents a paradigm shift in how we interact with our finances. Its potential to transform the financial industry and beyond is immense, offering new possibilities for innovation and growth. By addressing the challenges and leveraging the opportunities, we can shape a future where mobile banking contributes to a more inclusive, efficient, and sustainable global economy. For young people, understanding and engaging with these technologies can open up exciting career prospects and empower them to be active participants in the evolving landscape of finance.

7

Investing in the Digital Age

The digital age has revolutionized many aspects of our lives, and investing is no exception. The way we invest, the tools we use, and the opportunities available have all been transformed by technology. This chapter explores how young people can invest in the age of technology and fintech, the different investment options available, the risks and benefits of investing in emerging technologies, practical tips for investing wisely, and the impact of social media and online communities on investment decision-making.

The Rise of Digital Investing Platforms

In the past, investing was often seen as a complex and exclusive activity, accessible only to those with significant wealth and knowledge. Traditional investment methods involved working with financial advisors, brokers, and banks, often with high fees and minimum investment requirements. However, the rise of digital investing platforms has democratized access to investment opportunities, making it easier for individuals, especially young people, to start investing.

Digital investing platforms, such as Robinhood, E*TRADE, and Wealthfront, have made investing more accessible and affordable. These platforms offer user-friendly interfaces, low fees, and educational resources to help users make informed investment decisions. With just a smartphone or computer, individuals can buy and sell stocks, bonds, exchange-traded funds (ETFs), and other financial instruments with ease. The convenience and accessibility of these platforms have attracted millions of new investors, many of whom are young and new to the world of investing.

Types of Investment Options

The digital age has expanded the range of investment options available to individual investors. Some of the most popular investment options include:

Stocks:

1. Investing in individual stocks allows investors to buy shares of publicly traded companies. Stocks have the potential for high returns but also come with higher risk. Digital platforms provide access to a wide range of stocks from various industries and sectors.

Bonds:

1. Bonds are debt securities issued by governments, municipalities, and corporations to raise capital. They are considered lower risk compared to stocks and provide regular interest payments. Digital platforms offer access to a variety of bonds, including government bonds, corporate bonds, and municipal bonds.

Exchange-Traded Funds (ETFs):

1. ETFs are investment funds that trade on stock exchanges, similar to stocks. They offer diversification by holding a basket of securities, such as stocks, bonds, or commodities. ETFs are popular among investors

for their low fees and ease of trading.

Mutual Funds:

1. Mutual funds pool money from multiple investors to invest in a diversified portfolio of securities. They are managed by professional fund managers and offer diversification and professional management. Some digital platforms provide access to a wide range of mutual funds.

Real Estate Investment Trusts (REITs):

1. REITs allow investors to invest in real estate properties without directly owning them. They provide exposure to the real estate market and offer regular dividend payments. Digital platforms offer access to publicly traded REITs.

Cryptocurrencies:

1. Cryptocurrencies, such as Bitcoin and Ethereum, are digital assets that use blockchain technology for secure transactions. They have gained popularity as alternative investments, offering high potential returns but also significant volatility and risk.

Robo-Advisors:

1. Robo-advisors are digital platforms that use algorithms to provide investment advice and manage portfolios. They offer automated and personalized investment solutions, often at lower fees compared to traditional financial advisors. Examples of robo-advisors include Betterment and Wealthfront.

Peer-to-Peer Lending:

1. Peer-to-peer (P2P) lending platforms connect borrowers with individual lenders, bypassing traditional financial institutions. Investors can earn interest by lending money to borrowers. Examples of P2P lending platforms include LendingClub and Prosper.

Crowdfunding:

1. Crowdfunding platforms allow individuals to invest in startups and small businesses. Investors can participate in equity crowdfunding, where they receive shares in the company, or reward-based crowdfunding, where they receive products or services in return for their investment. Examples of crowdfunding platforms include Kickstarter and Indiegogo.

Benefits and Risks of Digital Investing

The digital age has brought numerous benefits to investing, but it also comes with risks that investors need to be aware of. Some of the key benefits of digital investing include:

Accessibility:

1. Digital platforms have made investing more accessible to a wider audience. With low fees, no minimum investment requirements, and user-friendly interfaces, more people can participate in the financial markets.

Convenience:

1. Digital investing allows users to manage their investments from anywhere at any time. Mobile apps and online platforms provide real-time access to account information, market data, and trading capabilities.

Education and Resources:

1. Many digital platforms offer educational resources, tools, and tutorials to help users learn about investing and make informed decisions. This empowers individuals to take control of their financial futures.

Automation:

1. Robo-advisors and automated investment tools simplify the investment process by providing personalized recommendations and managing portfolios on behalf of users. This can save time and reduce the complexity of investing.

Diversification:

1. Digital platforms offer access to a wide range of investment options, allowing users to diversify their portfolios and reduce risk. ETFs, mutual funds, and robo-advisors provide easy ways to achieve diversification.

Opportunities and Challenges

Investing in the digital age offers exciting opportunities, but it also comes with certain risks and challenges. One of the primary concerns is market volatility. Financial markets can be highly unpredictable, and investments may fluctuate in value. The ease of trading on digital platforms can lead to impulsive decisions, which might result in potential losses. Cybersecurity is another critical issue, as digital investing involves transmitting and storing sensitive financial information, making it a prime target for cybercriminals. Ensuring the security of personal and financial data is essential.

Digital platforms offer convenience and automation, but they might lack the personalized guidance and support provided by human financial advisors. Some investors might prefer a more hands-on approach. Additionally, the regulatory environment for digital investing is still evolving. Changes in regulations can impact the availability and operation of digital investment platforms. Overconfidence is another risk, especially among inexperienced investors who might assume they understand more than they do due to the ease of access provided by digital platforms.

Practical Tips for Investing Wisely

To navigate these challenges and invest wisely, it is essential to approach digital investing with a well-thought-out strategy. Start by setting clear financial goals. Whether you are saving for retirement, a down payment on a house, or a vacation, understanding your goals will help determine your investment horizon and risk tolerance. Diversification is another key principle. By spreading your investments across different asset classes, industries, and geographic regions, you can reduce risk and improve the potential for returns.

Conducting thorough research is vital for making informed investment decisions. Understand the fundamentals of the assets you are investing in, including their performance, risks, and potential for growth. Use the educational resources and tools provided by digital platforms to enhance your knowledge. For new investors, starting small and gradually increasing investments as you gain experience and confidence is a wise approach. This allows you to learn and adapt without taking on excessive risk.

Investing can be emotional, especially during periods of market volatility. It is important to stay disciplined and avoid making impulsive decisions based on fear or greed. Stick to your investment plan and long-term goals. Take advantage of automation and tools offered by digital platforms. Robo-advisors can provide personalized investment recommendations and manage your portfolio. Use budgeting and tracking tools to monitor your investments and stay on track with your financial goals.

The financial markets and investment landscape are constantly evolving. Stay informed about market trends, economic developments, and changes in regulations. Regularly review and adjust your investment strategy as needed. While digital platforms offer valuable resources and automation, there may be times when you need personalized advice from a financial professional. Do not hesitate to seek professional guidance if you have complex financial situations or specific investment questions.

The Impact of Social Media and Online Communities

Social media and online communities have significantly impacted investing in the digital age. Platforms like Reddit, Twitter, and YouTube have become popular sources of investment information, tips, and discussions. Online communities, such as Reddit's WallStreetBets, have even influenced market movements and created new trends in investing. Social media provides real-time access to a wealth of information, including market news, analyst opinions, and investment strategies. Investors can stay informed and up-to-date on the latest developments.

Online communities offer a sense of camaraderie and support among investors. Members can share experiences, ask questions, and provide encouragement, creating a collaborative environment. Social media platforms bring together investors from different backgrounds and expertise levels. This diversity of perspectives can provide valuable insights and broaden your understanding of investing. Online communities often engage in crowdsourced research and analysis. Members collaborate to analyze stocks, identify trends, and share findings, which can be beneficial for individual investors.

However, relying on social media and online communities for investment information comes with risks. Social media can be a source of misinformation and hype. Not all investment advice and tips shared online are accurate or reliable. It is important to verify information and conduct independent research. The influence of online communities can lead to herd mentality, where investors follow the crowd without fully understanding the underlying reasons. This can result in irrational decision-making and potential losses. Some individuals or groups may use social media to promote "pump and dump" schemes, where they artificially inflate the price of a stock and then sell it at a profit, leaving other investors with losses. Be cautious of investments that are heavily promoted online. Social media can amplify emotions, such as fear and greed, which can impact investment decisions. It is important to remain objective and stick to your investment plan.

Impact Investing and Socially Responsible Investing (SRI)

In the digital age, there has been a growing interest in impact investing and socially responsible investing (SRI). These investment approaches consider not only financial returns but also social and environmental impact. Digital platforms have made it easier for investors to align their investments with their values. Impact investing involves investing in companies, organizations, or funds that aim to generate positive social or environmental impact alongside financial returns. Examples include investing in renewable energy projects, affordable housing, or companies that promote gender equality. Socially responsible investing (SRI) involves selecting investments based on environmental, social, and governance (ESG) criteria. Investors use ESG factors to evaluate companies and avoid those that engage in harmful practices, such as polluting the environment, violating human rights, or lacking transparency.

Digital platforms and robo-advisors have developed tools to help investors incorporate impact investing and SRI into their portfolios. For example, some platforms allow users to filter investments based on ESG criteria, while others offer pre-built portfolios that focus on sustainability and social impact. Impact investing and SRI offer several benefits. These approaches allow investors to align their investments with their personal values and beliefs, supporting causes they care about. They aim to generate positive social and environmental outcomes, contributing to a better world. Companies that prioritize ESG factors are often better positioned for long-term success, as they are more resilient to risks and can attract socially conscious consumers and investors. Incorporating impact investments and SRI into your portfolio can provide diversification and reduce exposure to companies with harmful practices.

However, there are also challenges to consider. Some impact investments may prioritize social or environmental goals over financial returns, potentially leading to lower performance compared to traditional investments. Assessing the impact and performance of impact investments and SRI can be challenging due to the lack of standardized metrics and reporting practices. Some companies may engage in "greenwashing," where they exaggerate or misrepresent their commitment to ESG factors. It is important to conduct thorough research and verify claims.

The Role of Technology in Investment Decision-Making

Technology has transformed the way we make investment decisions by providing access to vast amounts of data, advanced analytics, and sophisticated tools. Digital platforms offer real-time market data, historical performance, and financial metrics, enabling investors to analyze data, identify trends, and make informed decisions. Algorithmic trading uses computer algorithms to execute trades based on predefined criteria, often outperforming human traders. Robo-advisors provide personalized investment recommendations and manage portfolios, considering factors like risk tolerance, investment horizon, and financial goals.

Predictive analytics uses statistical models and machine learning algorithms to forecast market trends and asset performance, helping investors make proactive decisions. Sentiment analysis uses natural language processing (NLP) to gauge market sentiment from news articles and social media posts, providing insights into investor behavior and market trends. Risk management tools help investors assess and manage investment risks through models, stress testing, and scenario analysis. Personal finance apps provide tools for budgeting, saving, and tracking investments, helping users stay organized and make better financial decisions.

Conclusion

Investing in the digital age offers numerous opportunities and advantages for young people. Digital investing platforms have democratized access to investment opportunities, making it easier and more affordable to start investing. A wide range of investment options, including stocks, bonds, ETFs, cryptocurrencies, and robo-advisors, allows for diversification and achieving financial goals.

However, digital investing also presents risks and challenges, such as market volatility, cybersecurity threats, and potential misinformation. It is essential to approach investing with caution, conduct thorough research, and develop a well-thought-out investment strategy. Social media and online communities offer access to information and support but also come with risks like misinformation and herd mentality. Impact investing and socially responsible investing (SRI) allow investors to align their investments with their values, promoting positive social and environmental outcomes. Technology has transformed investment decision-making by providing access to data, advanced analytics, and sophisticated tools, enabling informed decisions and effective risk management.

For young people, understanding and leveraging the opportunities offered by digital investing can provide valuable skills and financial empowerment. By staying informed about the latest trends and developments, young investors can make the most of opportunities in the digital age and contribute to a more inclusive, innovative, and sustainable financial system.

8

The Future of Finance

The future of finance is an exciting and dynamic field that is rapidly evolving due to technological advancements and changing consumer behaviors. As we look forward, it is evident that innovations such as artificial intelligence (AI), blockchain technology, decentralized finance (DeFi), quantum computing, and central bank digital currencies (CBDCs) will profoundly impact the financial industry. This chapter explores these technological advancements, the potential implications for young people and the broader economy, the challenges that arise as the financial industry continues to evolve, and provides recommendations for young people to prepare for the future of finance.

Artificial Intelligence (AI) and Machine Learning (ML) are already transforming the financial sector by enhancing efficiency, accuracy, and decision-making. These technologies are expected to play an even more significant role in the future. AI-powered algorithms can analyze vast amounts of data in real-time, providing insights into market trends, customer behavior, and investment opportunities. Machine learning models can continuously learn and adapt, improving their performance over time. For example, AI algorithms are used in high-frequency trading to make split-second decisions based on market data, which human traders could never match in speed and accuracy. Similarly, AI-driven credit scoring models can analyze a broader range of data points than traditional models, leading to more accurate assessments of credit risk and potentially making credit more accessible to a wider range of people.

AI is also likely to enhance customer service through the use of advanced chatbots and virtual assistants. These AI-powered tools can provide personalized support, answer complex queries, and offer tailored financial advice. As AI technology advances, these tools will become more sophisticated, providing a higher level of service to customers. For instance, a virtual assistant could not only help a customer manage their daily banking needs but also provide personalized investment advice based on the customer's financial goals and risk tolerance.

Blockchain technology, which underpins cryptocurrencies like Bitcoin and Ethereum, has the potential to revolutionize the financial industry by enabling secure, transparent, and decentralized transactions. One of the most promising applications of blockchain is in the realm of decentralized finance (DeFi). DeFi leverages blockchain technology to create open and permissionless financial systems that operate without traditional intermediaries like banks. DeFi platforms offer services such as lending, borrowing, trading, and asset management, all executed through smart contracts on the blockchain. This can make financial services more accessible, transparent, and efficient, but it also introduces new risks, such as smart contract vulnerabilities and regulatory uncertainties. For example, a DeFi lending platform could allow individuals to lend and borrow funds directly from each other, bypassing banks and potentially offering better terms due to lower overhead costs. However, the lack of regulation and the potential for software bugs in smart contracts pose significant risks that need to be managed.

Quantum computing represents another frontier in financial innovation. Quantum computers have the potential to solve complex problems much faster than classical computers, opening up new possibilities for financial modeling, risk management, and cryptography. Quantum computing could revolutionize areas such as portfolio optimization, derivative pricing, and fraud detection. For example, quantum algorithms could analyze vast datasets to identify optimal investment strategies that would be computationally infeasible with classical computers. Similarly, quantum cryptography could enhance the security of financial transactions by making it practically impossible for hackers to break encryption codes. However, the development and practical application of quantum computing in finance are still in their early stages. Significant technical challenges remain, and it may take several years before quantum computing becomes mainstream. Nevertheless, its potential impact on the financial industry is substantial.

Central banks around the world are exploring the development of central bank digital currencies (CBDCs). These digital currencies, issued and regulated by central banks, aim to complement existing monetary systems and provide a more efficient and secure means of payment. CBDCs can offer several benefits, including faster and cheaper transactions, enhanced financial inclusion, and improved monetary policy implementation. For example, CBDCs can provide a direct channel for distributing government payments and subsidies, reducing the need for intermediaries and ensuring that funds reach recipients quickly and securely. The adoption of CBDCs also presents challenges, such as ensuring privacy and security, addressing regulatory and legal issues, and managing the transition from traditional currencies. Central banks will need to carefully consider these factors as they develop and implement CBDCs.

The technological advancements shaping the future of finance have significant implications for young people and the broader economy. Understanding these implications can help young people navigate the evolving landscape and seize the opportunities it presents. As the financial industry evolves, the demand for new skills and job roles will increase. Young people with expertise in technology, data analysis, and cybersecurity will be well-positioned to pursue careers in the future financial industry.

Data analysis and data science skills will be crucial for making informed financial decisions and developing AI and ML models. The ability to analyze and interpret large datasets will become increasingly important as financial institutions rely on data-driven insights to drive their strategies and operations. For example, data scientists in the financial sector might develop predictive models to forecast market trends or assess the creditworthiness of loan applicants using machine learning techniques. Cybersecurity skills will also be in high demand, as ensuring the security of financial systems and data will be a top priority. With the rise of digital banking and online transactions, the need to protect against cyber threats and data breaches will become even more critical.

Another important area of expertise will be blockchain and distributed ledger technology. Understanding how blockchain works and its potential applications in finance will open up new career opportunities in areas such as blockchain development, smart contract programming, and decentralized finance. As blockchain technology continues to evolve, professionals with the skills to implement and manage blockchain solutions will be highly sought after. For example, blockchain developers might create decentralized applications (dApps) that facilitate peer-to-peer lending or automate complex financial contracts through smart contracts.

The integration of AI and automation into financial services will also create new job roles and opportunities. While some traditional roles may be automated, new roles will emerge that focus on developing, managing, and overseeing AI systems. Professionals with a strong understanding of AI ethics, algorithmic transparency, and the regulatory implications of AI will be essential in ensuring that AI systems are used responsibly and ethically. For instance, AI ethicists might work to ensure that algorithms used in lending do not inadvertently discriminate against certain demographic groups.

In addition to technical skills, soft skills such as communication, problem-solving, and adaptability will remain important. The ability to collaborate with cross-functional teams, communicate complex ideas clearly, and adapt to rapidly changing technologies and market conditions will be valuable in the future financial industry. For example, financial professionals will need to work closely with IT and data science teams to implement new technologies effectively and ensure they meet the needs of clients and regulators.

The future of finance will also have broader economic implications. Technological advancements have the potential to drive economic growth by increasing efficiency, reducing costs, and creating new business opportunities. For example, AI and automation can streamline operations, reduce manual processes, and improve decision-making, leading to cost savings and increased productivity. Blockchain technology can enhance transparency and trust in financial transactions, reducing the need for intermediaries and lowering transaction costs. For instance, a blockchain-based system for cross-border payments could significantly reduce the time and cost associated with international money transfers.

However, these advancements also present challenges and risks. The rapid pace of technological change can lead to job displacement and economic disruption. As certain tasks and roles become automated, workers may need to acquire new skills and transition to different roles. Ensuring that the workforce is prepared for these changes through education and reskilling programs will be crucial in mitigating the impact of job displacement. Governments, educational institutions, and private companies will need to collaborate to provide training and support for workers affected by technological disruption.

Regulation will play a critical role in shaping the future of finance. As new technologies emerge, regulators will need to develop frameworks that balance innovation with consumer protection and financial stability. Clear and consistent regulations can provide stability and encourage investment in new technologies while protecting consumers from potential risks. For example, regulations for AI in finance might require transparency in algorithmic decision-making to prevent discrimination and ensure fairness.

The adoption of new technologies also raises ethical considerations. Ensuring that AI and automation are used responsibly and ethically will be essential. Issues such as algorithmic bias, data privacy, and transparency must be addressed to build trust and ensure that technological advancements benefit all stakeholders. For instance, financial institutions using AI for credit scoring must ensure that their algorithms do not inadvertently perpetuate biases against certain demographic groups.

For young people, preparing for the future of finance involves staying informed about technological advancements, developing relevant skills, and being adaptable to change. Keeping up with the latest trends and developments in finance and technology can provide valuable insights and opportunities for career growth. Developing technical skills in areas such as data analysis, cybersecurity, and blockchain will be important, but so will honing soft skills such as communication, problem-solving, and adaptability.

Educational institutions, professional organizations, and online platforms offer a wide range of resources and courses to help young people develop these skills. Participating in internships, attending industry conferences, and joining professional networks can also provide valuable experience and connections. For example, students might participate in a summer internship at a fintech company to gain hands-on experience with blockchain technology or AI-driven financial services.

Understanding the ethical and regulatory implications of new technologies will be important for navigating the future financial landscape. Being aware of the potential risks and challenges and staying informed about regulatory developments can help young people make informed decisions and contribute to the responsible and ethical use of technology in finance. For instance, young professionals might engage with industry groups or regulatory bodies to stay abreast of new regulations and best practices.

The rise of decentralized finance (DeFi) represents one of the most exciting and transformative trends in the future of finance. DeFi platforms, built on blockchain technology, aim to recreate traditional financial systems in a decentralized manner. This means that users can lend, borrow, trade, and invest without relying on traditional financial intermediaries like banks. Instead, these transactions are facilitated by smart contracts—self-executing contracts with the terms of the agreement directly written into code.

One of the primary benefits of DeFi is that it can increase financial inclusion by providing access to financial services for individuals who are unbanked or underbanked. In many parts of the world, access to traditional banking services is limited by factors such as geographic location, economic status, or political instability. DeFi platforms can be accessed by anyone with an internet connection, allowing users to participate in the global financial system regardless of their location or economic status.

Moreover, DeFi can offer greater transparency and security compared to traditional financial systems. All transactions on a DeFi platform are recorded on a public blockchain, which can be audited by anyone. This level of transparency can reduce the risk of fraud and corruption. Additionally, because DeFi platforms operate on decentralized networks, they are less vulnerable to systemic failures or attacks that could compromise centralized financial institutions.

However, DeFi is not without its challenges. One of the primary risks associated with DeFi is the potential for smart contract vulnerabilities. Smart contracts are complex pieces of code, and if there are bugs or flaws in the code, they can be exploited by malicious actors. There have been several high-profile cases of DeFi platforms being hacked, resulting in significant financial losses for users. Therefore, ensuring the security and reliability of smart contracts is crucial for the long-term success of DeFi.

Another challenge is the regulatory uncertainty surrounding DeFi. Because

DeFi operates outside of traditional financial systems, it is often not subject to the same regulations as traditional financial institutions. This can create legal and compliance risks for users and developers of DeFi platforms. Regulators around the world are still grappling with how to approach DeFi, and it is likely that the regulatory landscape will continue to evolve in the coming years.

Quantum computing is another technology that has the potential to revolutionize the financial industry. Unlike classical computers, which use bits to process information, quantum computers use quantum bits, or qubits. Qubits can exist in multiple states simultaneously, allowing quantum computers to perform many calculations at once. This makes quantum computers particularly well-suited for solving complex problems that are beyond the capabilities of classical computers.

In finance, quantum computing could be used to optimize investment portfolios, model financial markets, and develop new cryptographic techniques to enhance security. For example, quantum algorithms could be used to identify the optimal combination of assets in a portfolio, taking into account a wide range of factors such as market conditions, risk tolerance, and investment goals. Similarly, quantum computers could be used to develop more accurate models of financial markets, helping traders and investors make better-informed decisions.

However, the practical application of quantum computing in finance is still in its early stages. There are significant technical challenges that need to be overcome, and it may be several years before quantum computing becomes mainstream. Nevertheless, its potential impact on the financial industry is substantial, and it is an area that young people interested in finance and technology should keep an eye on.

The development of central bank digital currencies (CBDCs) is another trend that could have a significant impact on the future of finance. CBDCs are digital versions of a country's national currency, issued and regulated by the central bank. Unlike cryptocurrencies like Bitcoin, which are decentralized and operate independently of any central authority, CBDCs are centralized and backed by the government.

CBDCs have the potential to provide several benefits, including faster and cheaper transactions, enhanced financial inclusion, and improved monetary policy implementation. For example, CBDCs could enable real-time settlement of payments, reducing the time and cost associated with traditional payment systems. This could be particularly beneficial for cross-border transactions, which are often slow and expensive due to the involvement of multiple intermediaries.

CBDCs could also enhance financial inclusion by providing access to digital financial services for individuals who are unbanked or underbanked. In many developing countries, access to traditional banking services is limited, and cash is the primary means of payment. CBDCs could provide a digital alternative to cash, allowing individuals to participate in the digital economy and access a wider range of financial services.

Moreover, CBDCs could improve the effectiveness of monetary policy by providing central banks with more direct control over the money supply. For example, central banks could use CBDCs to implement negative interest rates, where money held in digital wallets loses value over time, encouraging people to spend rather than save. This could be a powerful tool for stimulating economic activity during periods of low growth or recession.

However, the development and implementation of CBDCs also present several challenges. One of the primary concerns is ensuring the privacy and security of CBDC transactions. Because CBDCs are digital, they are vulnerable to cyberattacks and data breaches. Ensuring the security of the underlying technology and protecting users' privacy will be critical for the success of CBDCs.

Another challenge is managing the transition from traditional currencies to CBDCs. This transition will require significant changes to the existing financial infrastructure and could have wide-ranging implications for banks, businesses, and consumers. Central banks will need to carefully consider these factors as they develop and implement CBDCs.

The future of finance will also be shaped by the ongoing evolution of financial markets and institutions. Traditional financial institutions, such as banks and insurance companies, are increasingly adopting new technologies to enhance their services and remain competitive. For example, many banks are investing in digital transformation initiatives to improve their online and mobile banking platforms, streamline operations, and offer new products and services.

At the same time, new players are entering the financial industry, leveraging technology to offer innovative financial services. Fintech startups are developing new solutions for payments, lending, wealth management, and insurance, challenging traditional financial institutions and driving competition. This dynamic and competitive environment is fostering innovation and providing consumers with a wider range of choices.

For young people, preparing for the future of finance involves staying informed about technological advancements, developing relevant skills, and being adaptable to change. Keeping up with the latest trends and developments in finance and technology can provide valuable insights and opportunities for career growth. Developing technical skills in areas such as data analysis, cybersecurity, and blockchain will be important, but so will honing soft skills such as communication, problem-solving, and adaptability.

Educational institutions, professional organizations, and online platforms offer a wide range of resources and courses to help young people develop these skills. Participating in internships, attending industry conferences, and joining professional networks can also provide valuable experience and connections. For example, students might participate in a summer internship at a fintech company to gain hands-on experience with blockchain technology or AI-driven financial services.

Understanding the ethical and regulatory implications of new technologies will be important for navigating the future financial landscape. Being aware of the potential risks and challenges, and staying informed about regulatory developments, can help young people make informed decisions and contribute to the responsible and ethical use of technology in finance. For instance, young professionals might engage with industry groups or regulatory bodies to stay abreast of new regulations and best practices.

In conclusion, the future of finance will be shaped by several key technological advancements, including artificial intelligence, blockchain technology, decentralized finance, quantum computing, and central bank digital currencies. These technologies have the potential to revolutionize the financial industry, creating new opportunities and challenges. For young people, understanding these technologies and their implications will be essential for navigating the evolving financial landscape and seizing the opportunities it presents. Developing relevant technical and soft skills, staying informed about industry trends, and being adaptable to change will be crucial for success in the future of finance. By preparing for these changes, young people can contribute to the development of a more inclusive, innovative, and sustainable financial system.

9

Regulatory Challenges in Fintech

As fintech continues to grow and transform the financial landscape, it faces a myriad of regulatory challenges. The rapid pace of innovation in financial technology often outstrips the ability of regulatory frameworks to keep up. This chapter explores the complexities of regulatory compliance in fintech, the impact of regulatory hurdles on innovation, and strategies for achieving and maintaining compliance. It also discusses the role of regulatory bodies and the importance of collaboration between fintech companies and regulators.

Fintech, which encompasses a wide range of financial technologies including mobile banking, peer-to-peer lending, robo-advisors, and blockchain, operates in a highly regulated environment. Traditional financial services are subject to extensive regulations designed to protect consumers, ensure market stability, and prevent financial crimes. As fintech companies enter the financial services space, they must navigate these regulations, which can be complex and vary widely across different jurisdictions.

One of the primary regulatory challenges for fintech companies is ensuring compliance with anti-money laundering (AML) and know-your-customer (KYC) regulations. AML regulations are designed to prevent money laundering and terrorist financing by requiring financial institutions to implement robust measures to detect and report suspicious activities. KYC regulations, on the other hand, require financial institutions to verify the identity of their customers and assess the risks of illegal activities associated with them.

For fintech companies, complying with AML and KYC regulations can be particularly challenging. Unlike traditional banks, which have established processes and infrastructure for compliance, fintech startups may lack the resources and expertise to implement comprehensive AML and KYC programs. Additionally, fintech companies often operate in a digital environment where transactions occur online and customer interactions are remote, making it more difficult to verify identities and detect suspicious activities.

To address these challenges, many fintech companies are turning to technology-driven solutions. For example, they are using AI and machine learning algorithms to analyze transaction data and identify patterns indicative of money laundering. These technologies can enhance the accuracy and efficiency of AML compliance by automating the detection of suspicious activities and reducing false positives. Similarly, fintech companies are employing digital identity verification technologies, such as biometric authentication and document verification, to streamline the KYC process and ensure compliance.

Another significant regulatory challenge for fintech companies is data privacy and protection. The digital nature of fintech services means that vast amounts of sensitive financial and personal data are collected, processed, and stored. Ensuring the security and privacy of this data is crucial to maintaining customer trust and complying with data protection regulations, such as the General Data Protection Regulation (GDPR) in the European Union and the California Consumer Privacy Act (CCPA) in the United States.

Data protection regulations impose stringent requirements on how fintech companies handle personal data. These include obtaining explicit consent from customers before collecting their data, ensuring the data is used only for specified purposes, and implementing robust security measures to protect against data breaches. Compliance with these regulations can be complex and resource-intensive, particularly for small fintech startups.

To navigate data privacy challenges, fintech companies must prioritize data protection from the outset. This involves implementing privacy-by-design principles, where data protection measures are integrated into the development and operation of products and services. Additionally, fintech companies should conduct regular risk assessments, employ encryption and other security technologies, and establish clear policies and procedures for data handling and breach response.

The regulatory landscape for fintech is continually evolving, with new regulations and guidelines being introduced to address emerging risks and challenges. For example, the rise of cryptocurrencies and blockchain technology has prompted regulators to develop specific regulations for these areas. Cryptocurrencies, such as Bitcoin and Ethereum, operate in a decentralized manner, often outside the traditional financial system. This has raised concerns about their potential use for illegal activities, such as money laundering and terrorist financing, as well as the risks they pose to financial stability and consumer protection.

In response, regulators around the world are developing frameworks to regulate cryptocurrencies and their associated activities. These frameworks typically address issues such as registration and licensing requirements for cryptocurrency exchanges, AML and KYC obligations, and consumer protection measures. However, the regulatory approaches vary widely across different jurisdictions, creating challenges for fintech companies that operate internationally.

For example, in the United States, the Securities and Exchange Commission (SEC) has taken a proactive approach to regulating cryptocurrencies, classifying certain digital tokens as securities and subjecting them to securities laws. The Financial Crimes Enforcement Network (FinCEN) has also issued guidance on the application of AML regulations to cryptocurrency exchanges and other virtual asset service providers. In contrast, countries like Japan and Switzerland have adopted more favorable regulatory environments for cryptocurrencies, recognizing them as legitimate financial instruments and providing clear guidelines for their operation.

The regulatory diversity across jurisdictions creates compliance challenges for fintech companies that operate globally. These companies must navigate different regulatory requirements, often adapting their operations and compliance programs to meet the specific regulations of each jurisdiction. This can be resource-intensive and complex, requiring a deep understanding of the regulatory landscape and ongoing monitoring of regulatory developments.

Despite the challenges, regulatory compliance is crucial for the success and sustainability of fintech companies. Non-compliance can result in significant legal and financial consequences, including fines, sanctions, and reputational damage. It can also hinder the ability of fintech companies to attract investment and partner with traditional financial institutions.

To achieve and maintain compliance, fintech companies should adopt a proactive and strategic approach to regulation. This involves staying informed about regulatory developments, engaging with regulators and industry bodies, and investing in compliance infrastructure and expertise. Building strong relationships with regulators and participating in regulatory consultations and initiatives can also help fintech companies influence the development of regulations and ensure they are practical and supportive of innovation.

One effective strategy for achieving compliance is the implementation of a robust governance, risk, and compliance (GRC) framework. A GRC framework provides a structured approach to managing regulatory requirements, risks, and controls. It involves identifying and assessing regulatory obligations, implementing policies and procedures to ensure compliance, and continuously monitoring and reporting on compliance activities.

Technology can play a critical role in supporting GRC efforts. Regtech, short for regulatory technology, refers to the use of technology to enhance regulatory compliance and risk management. Regtech solutions can automate compliance processes, such as transaction monitoring, reporting, and risk assessments, reducing the administrative burden and improving the accuracy and efficiency of compliance activities. For example, AI-driven regtech solutions can analyze large volumes of transaction data in real-time to detect suspicious activities and generate automated reports for regulatory authorities.

Collaboration and information sharing between fintech companies and regulators are essential for addressing regulatory challenges and fostering innovation. Regulatory sandboxes are one approach that has gained popularity in recent years. A regulatory sandbox is a controlled environment where fintech companies can test new products and services under the supervision of regulators. This allows companies to experiment and innovate while ensuring compliance with regulatory requirements.

Regulatory sandboxes provide several benefits. They enable fintech companies to gain valuable feedback from regulators and refine their products and services before launching them to the broader market. They also allow regulators to better understand emerging technologies and their implications, facilitating the development of informed and balanced regulations. By fostering a collaborative approach, regulatory sandboxes can promote innovation while ensuring that consumer protection and financial stability are maintained.

The importance of consumer protection in fintech cannot be overstated. As fintech companies introduce new products and services, they must ensure that consumers are adequately informed and protected. This involves providing clear and transparent information about the products and services, including their risks and benefits. It also involves implementing measures to prevent and address consumer complaints and disputes.

One of the key areas of consumer protection in fintech is ensuring fair and transparent pricing. Fintech companies must clearly disclose all fees and charges associated with their products and services, ensuring that consumers understand the costs involved. They must also avoid deceptive marketing practices and provide accurate information about the performance and risks of investment products.

Financial literacy is another important aspect of consumer protection. Fintech companies should provide educational resources and tools to help consumers make informed financial decisions. This includes offering information on how to use fintech products and services effectively, as well as providing guidance on broader financial topics such as budgeting, saving, and investing.

Addressing the challenges of digital inclusion is also critical for consumer protection in fintech. While fintech has the potential to enhance financial inclusion, it also risks excluding individuals who lack access to digital technologies or the skills to use them. Fintech companies must ensure that their products and services are accessible to all consumers, regardless of their digital literacy or socioeconomic status. This may involve providing alternative access channels, such as phone-based services, and offering support and training to help consumers use digital platforms.

In conclusion, the regulatory challenges facing fintech are complex and multifaceted. Ensuring compliance with AML, KYC, data privacy, and other regulations is critical for the success and sustainability of fintech companies. As the regulatory landscape continues to evolve, fintech companies must adopt proactive and strategic approaches to compliance, leveraging technology and collaboration to navigate the regulatory environment effectively. By prioritizing consumer protection, transparency, and digital inclusion, fintech companies can build trust and confidence in their products and services, fostering innovation and contributing to the development of a more inclusive and resilient financial system.

10

Sustainable Finance and ESG Investing

The world of finance is increasingly recognizing the importance of sustainability and the need to address environmental, social, and governance (ESG) issues. Sustainable finance and ESG investing are becoming central to financial strategies, driven by growing awareness of climate change, social inequalities, and corporate governance issues. This chapter explores the principles of sustainable finance, the trends in impact investing, the incorporation of ESG criteria into investment decisions, and the challenges and opportunities associated with these practices.

Sustainable finance is an approach to financial decision-making that considers the long-term environmental, social, and economic impacts of investments. It aims to foster economic growth while ensuring that environmental and social needs are met, contributing to the overall well-being of society. Sustainable finance encompasses a wide range of financial products and services, including green bonds, social impact bonds, and sustainability-linked loans.

ESG investing, a key component of sustainable finance, involves integrating environmental, social, and governance factors into investment decisions. Environmental criteria consider how a company's operations impact the environment, including issues such as carbon emissions, resource depletion, and waste management. Social criteria examine how a company manages relationships with employees, suppliers, customers, and communities, addressing issues like labor practices, human rights, and community engagement. Governance criteria assess a company's leadership, executive pay, audits, internal controls, and shareholder rights.

The rise of ESG investing reflects a broader shift in the financial industry towards more responsible and ethical investment practices. Investors are increasingly recognizing that ESG factors can have a significant impact on the financial performance and long-term sustainability of companies. By incorporating ESG criteria into their investment strategies, investors aim to identify companies that are well-positioned to manage risks and capitalize on opportunities related to environmental and social challenges.

One of the driving forces behind the growth of ESG investing is the increasing awareness of climate change and its potential economic impacts. Climate change poses significant risks to the global economy, including physical risks such as extreme weather events and transition risks associated with the shift to a low-carbon economy. Investors are increasingly seeking to mitigate these risks by investing in companies that are proactively addressing climate change and reducing their carbon footprint.

For example, many investors are now considering the carbon intensity of their portfolios and seeking to reduce exposure to high-carbon industries such as fossil fuels. This has led to the growth of green bonds, which are bonds specifically earmarked to finance projects that have positive environmental benefits. Green bonds can be used to fund renewable energy projects, energy efficiency improvements, and other initiatives that contribute to the transition to a sustainable economy.

Social issues are also becoming a key focus for ESG investors. Companies are increasingly being scrutinized for their social impact, including how they treat their employees, the diversity and inclusion practices they adopt, and their engagement with local communities. Investors are looking for companies that demonstrate strong social responsibility and are committed to ethical business practices. This includes issues such as fair labor practices, human rights, and community development.

Governance is the third pillar of ESG investing, focusing on the structures and processes that ensure a company is managed in the best interests of its stakeholders. Good governance practices are essential for building trust and transparency, and they can have a significant impact on a company's reputation and financial performance. Investors are looking for companies with strong governance frameworks, including effective boards of directors, transparent reporting practices, and mechanisms to prevent corruption and unethical behavior.

The growth of ESG investing is being driven by several key trends. One of the most significant trends is the increasing demand for transparency and accountability from investors. Investors are seeking more detailed and standardized information on how companies are managing ESG risks and opportunities. This has led to the development of ESG reporting frameworks and standards, such as the Global Reporting Initiative (GRI) and the Sustainability Accounting Standards Board (SASB), which provide guidelines for companies to disclose their ESG performance.

Another trend is the rise of impact investing, which involves making investments with the intention of generating positive social or environmental impact alongside financial returns. Impact investing goes beyond traditional ESG investing by actively seeking to create measurable positive outcomes. This approach is gaining popularity among investors who want to make a difference and contribute to solving global challenges such as poverty, inequality, and climate change.

Impact investing can take various forms, including investments in social enterprises, community development finance institutions, and impact funds.

These investments are typically directed towards projects and organizations that address specific social or environmental issues, such as affordable housing, clean energy, and sustainable agriculture. Impact investors often use metrics and benchmarks to measure and report on the social and environmental impact of their investments, ensuring transparency and accountability.

The growth of sustainable finance and ESG investing is also being supported by regulatory developments. Governments and regulatory bodies around the world are introducing policies and regulations to promote sustainability and responsible investment practices. For example, the European Union's Sustainable Finance Disclosure Regulation (SFDR) requires financial market participants to disclose how they integrate ESG factors into their investment decisions. Similarly, the Task Force on Climate-related Financial Disclosures (TCFD) provides recommendations for companies to disclose climate-related financial risks and opportunities.

Despite the positive momentum, there are several challenges associated with sustainable finance and ESG investing. One of the primary challenges is the lack of standardized and comparable ESG data. While there are various reporting frameworks and standards, the quality and consistency of ESG data can vary significantly between companies. This makes it difficult for investors to assess and compare the ESG performance of different companies accurately.

Another challenge is the potential for greenwashing, where companies exaggerate or misrepresent their ESG practices to appear more sustainable than they are. Greenwashing can undermine the credibility of ESG investing and make it challenging for investors to identify genuinely sustainable companies. To address this issue, there is a growing need for rigorous verification and assurance processes to ensure the accuracy and reliability of ESG disclosures.

SUSTAINABLE FINANCE AND ESG INVESTING

The incorporation of ESG criteria into investment decisions also requires a shift in mindset and culture within financial institutions. Traditional investment approaches often focus on short-term financial performance, whereas ESG investing requires a longer-term perspective that considers non-financial factors. This shift requires education and training for investment professionals, as well as changes in incentive structures to align with ESG goals.

Despite these challenges, the opportunities associated with sustainable finance and ESG investing are significant. Companies that proactively manage ESG risks and opportunities are likely to be better positioned for long-term success. They can enhance their reputation, attract and retain talent, and build stronger relationships with customers and stakeholders. Additionally, by addressing social and environmental challenges, these companies can contribute to a more sustainable and equitable world.

For young people interested in finance, understanding sustainable finance and ESG investing is crucial. The demand for professionals with expertise in ESG is growing, and developing skills in this area can open up exciting career opportunities. Financial analysts, portfolio managers, and investment advisors with knowledge of ESG factors will be in high demand as the industry continues to evolve.

To prepare for a career in sustainable finance, young people should seek to build a strong foundation in finance and economics while also gaining knowledge of environmental and social issues. Courses and certifications in sustainable finance, such as the CFA Institute's Certificate in ESG Investing, can provide valuable credentials and enhance job prospects. Additionally, gaining practical experience through internships and involvement in sustainability initiatives can provide hands-on learning and networking opportunities.

Incorporating ESG factors into investment decisions also requires a holistic understanding of the interconnectedness of financial, environmental, and social systems. Young professionals should develop critical thinking and analytical skills to assess the broader impacts of investment decisions. They should also stay informed about the latest developments in sustainable finance, including emerging trends, regulatory changes, and best practices.

As the demand for transparency and accountability continues to grow, technology will play an increasingly important role in sustainable finance. Advanced data analytics, artificial intelligence, and blockchain technology can enhance ESG data collection, analysis, and reporting. For example, AI-driven analytics can help investors identify ESG risks and opportunities by analyzing large datasets from various sources. Blockchain technology can provide a secure and transparent way to track and verify ESG-related information, reducing the risk of greenwashing and ensuring data integrity.

Sustainable finance and ESG investing represent a fundamental shift in the financial industry towards more responsible and ethical practices. By considering the long-term impacts of investments on the environment and society, investors can contribute to a more sustainable and equitable world. For young people, understanding and engaging with these practices can provide valuable skills and career opportunities, as well as the chance to make a positive impact on the world.

In conclusion, sustainable finance and ESG investing are reshaping the financial landscape by integrating environmental, social, and governance factors into investment decisions. The growing awareness of climate change, social inequalities, and corporate governance issues is driving demand for more responsible and ethical investment practices. While challenges such as data quality, greenwashing, and the need for a cultural shift within financial institutions remain, the opportunities for positive impact and long-term value creation are significant. By developing expertise in sustainable finance and ESG investing, young professionals can contribute to the development of a more sustainable and resilient financial system.

11

Cybersecurity in Finance

As the financial industry becomes increasingly digital, the importance of cybersecurity cannot be overstated. Financial institutions handle vast amounts of sensitive data, including personal and financial information, making them prime targets for cybercriminals. This chapter explores the cybersecurity risks facing the financial industry, strategies for protecting data, incident response and recovery, and the role of regulatory frameworks in enhancing cybersecurity.

The digital transformation of finance has brought numerous benefits, such as improved efficiency, enhanced customer experiences, and greater accessibility. However, it has also introduced new vulnerabilities and threats. Cyberattacks on financial institutions can result in significant financial losses, damage to reputation, and regulatory penalties. The stakes are high, and ensuring robust cybersecurity measures is essential for maintaining trust and stability in the financial system.

One of the primary cybersecurity risks facing the financial industry is data breaches. Cybercriminals often target financial institutions to steal sensitive data, such as customer account information, credit card details, and Social Security numbers. This data can be used for identity theft, fraud, and other malicious activities. Data breaches can occur through various means, including hacking, phishing attacks, and insider threats.

To protect against data breaches, financial institutions must implement a comprehensive security strategy that includes multiple layers of defense. Encryption is a critical component of data protection, ensuring that sensitive information is encrypted both in transit and at rest. This makes it difficult for unauthorized parties to access and decipher the data even if they intercept it.

Multi-factor authentication (MFA) is another essential security measure. MFA requires users to provide multiple forms of identification, such as a password and a one-time code sent to their mobile device, before accessing an account. This adds an extra layer of security, making it more challenging for cybercriminals to gain unauthorized access.

Regular security assessments and vulnerability testing are crucial for identifying and addressing potential weaknesses in the system. Financial institutions should conduct penetration testing, where ethical hackers attempt to breach the system to uncover vulnerabilities. These tests help identify areas that need improvement and ensure that security measures are up to date.

Employee training and awareness are also vital components of a robust cybersecurity strategy. Human error is often a significant factor in security breaches, with employees inadvertently clicking on malicious links or falling victim to phishing scams. Regular training programs can educate employees about cybersecurity best practices, how to recognize and respond to potential threats, and the importance of maintaining a security-conscious mindset.

Incident response and recovery are critical aspects of cybersecurity in finance. Despite the best efforts to prevent cyberattacks, incidents can still occur. Having a well-defined incident response plan is essential for minimizing the impact of a cyberattack and ensuring a swift recovery. An effective incident response plan should include clear procedures for detecting and reporting incidents, roles and responsibilities for the response team, and steps for containing and mitigating the attack.

One of the first steps in incident response is to identify the scope and nature of the attack. This involves analyzing logs, network traffic, and other indicators to determine how the attack occurred, what systems and data were affected, and the extent of the damage. Once the scope of the attack is understood, the next step is to contain it to prevent further damage. This may involve isolating affected systems, blocking malicious IP addresses, and disabling compromised accounts.

After containing the attack, the focus shifts to eradicating the threat. This involves removing malware, patching vulnerabilities, and restoring affected systems from backups. Ensuring that all traces of the attack are eliminated is crucial to prevent a recurrence. Once the threat is eradicated, the recovery phase begins, which involves restoring normal operations and addressing any residual impacts.

Communication is a critical component of incident response. Financial institutions must communicate with affected customers, regulators, and other stakeholders to inform them about the incident and the steps being taken to address it. Transparency and timely communication can help maintain trust and mitigate the reputational damage associated with a cyberattack.

In addition to incident response, financial institutions must also focus on building resilience to cyber threats. This involves implementing measures to ensure that critical systems and data can continue to operate even in the face of an attack. Business continuity planning and disaster recovery are key components of building resilience. These plans should outline procedures for maintaining operations and recovering from disruptions, including cyberattacks.

Cyber insurance is another tool that financial institutions can use to mitigate the financial impact of a cyberattack. Cyber insurance policies can provide coverage for various costs associated with a cyber incident, such as legal fees, notification costs, and business interruption losses. However, it is essential to carefully review and understand the terms and conditions of the policy to ensure that it provides adequate coverage for the specific risks faced by the institution.

Regulatory frameworks play a crucial role in enhancing cybersecurity in the financial industry. Regulators around the world have introduced various guidelines and requirements to ensure that financial institutions implement robust cybersecurity measures. For example, the European Union's General Data Protection Regulation (GDPR) imposes strict requirements on data protection and breach notification. Similarly, the New York Department of Financial Services (NYDFS) has implemented cybersecurity regulations that require financial institutions to establish and maintain comprehensive cybersecurity programs.

Compliance with regulatory requirements is essential for financial institutions to avoid legal and financial penalties. However, regulatory compliance should be viewed as a baseline rather than the ultimate goal. Financial institutions should strive to exceed regulatory requirements and adopt a proactive approach to cybersecurity, continuously assessing and improving their security measures.

Collaboration and information sharing are also critical for enhancing cybersecurity in the financial industry. Cyber threats are constantly evolving, and no single institution can address these challenges alone. Financial institutions should collaborate with industry peers, government agencies, and cybersecurity organizations to share information about threats, vulnerabilities, and best practices. Initiatives such as the Financial Services Information Sharing and Analysis Center (FS-ISAC) provide a platform for information sharing and collaboration within the financial sector.

Emerging technologies, such as artificial intelligence (AI) and machine learning (ML), offer new opportunities for enhancing cybersecurity in finance. AI and ML can analyze vast amounts of data in real-time to detect and respond to threats more quickly and accurately. For example, AI-driven security systems can identify unusual patterns of behavior that may indicate a cyberattack and automatically initiate response measures. Similarly, ML algorithms can continuously learn and adapt to new threats, improving their effectiveness over time.

Blockchain technology also holds promise for enhancing cybersecurity in finance. The decentralized and immutable nature of blockchain can provide a secure and transparent way to record and verify transactions, reducing the risk of fraud and tampering. Blockchain can be used to enhance the security of various financial processes, such as identity verification, transaction settlement, and supply chain management.

Despite the potential benefits, the adoption of emerging technologies also introduces new cybersecurity challenges. For example, AI and ML systems can be vulnerable to adversarial attacks, where malicious actors manipulate the input data to deceive the algorithms. Similarly, the complexity of blockchain technology can create new attack vectors that need to be addressed. Financial institutions must carefully evaluate the risks and benefits of emerging technologies and implement appropriate security measures to mitigate these risks.

For young people interested in pursuing a career in finance, understanding cybersecurity is essential. The demand for cybersecurity professionals in the financial industry is growing, and developing skills in this area can open up exciting career opportunities. Key skills for cybersecurity professionals include knowledge of network security, encryption, incident response, and risk management. Additionally, staying informed about the latest cybersecurity trends and developments is crucial for staying ahead of emerging threats.

Educational institutions, professional organizations, and online platforms offer a wide range of resources and courses to help young people develop cybersecurity skills. Certifications such as Certified Information Systems Security Professional (CISSP) and Certified Ethical Hacker (CEH) can provide valuable credentials and enhance job prospects. Gaining practical experience through internships and involvement in cybersecurity initiatives can also provide hands-on learning and networking opportunities.

In the rapidly evolving field of cybersecurity, staying up-to-date with the latest technologies and threats is crucial. Cybersecurity professionals must engage in continuous learning and professional development to keep pace with the changing landscape. This includes attending industry conferences, participating in training programs, and obtaining advanced certifications.

The role of a cybersecurity professional in the financial industry is multifaceted. It involves not only technical expertise but also strategic thinking and effective communication. Cybersecurity professionals must work closely with other departments, such as IT, risk management, and compliance, to develop and implement comprehensive security strategies. They must also communicate complex technical concepts to non-technical stakeholders, including senior management and regulators, to ensure a shared understanding of cybersecurity risks and mitigation measures.

A key aspect of a cybersecurity professional's role is conducting risk assessments to identify potential threats and vulnerabilities. This involves evaluating the organization's systems, networks, and processes to determine where weaknesses exist and what impact they could have. Risk assessments should be conducted regularly and updated to reflect changes in the threat landscape and the organization's operations.

Another important responsibility is developing and implementing security policies and procedures. These policies should outline the organization's approach to cybersecurity, including acceptable use of technology, data protection, incident response, and employee training. Clear and comprehensive policies are essential for ensuring that all employees understand their roles and responsibilities in maintaining security.

Cybersecurity professionals must also stay vigilant for signs of potential threats. This includes monitoring network traffic, analyzing security logs, and using intrusion detection systems to identify suspicious activities. Early detection of threats is crucial for preventing or minimizing the impact of cyberattacks.

When a security incident occurs, cybersecurity professionals play a critical role in responding to and mitigating the attack. This involves following the incident response plan, coordinating with the response team, and implementing measures to contain and eradicate the threat. Effective incident response requires a combination of technical skills, strategic thinking, and clear communication.

Recovery from a cyberattack involves not only restoring affected systems but also addressing the root causes of the incident to prevent future occurrences. This may include updating security measures, conducting post-incident reviews, and implementing lessons learned. Cybersecurity professionals must work with other departments to ensure that recovery efforts are comprehensive and effective.

Regulatory compliance is another critical aspect of cybersecurity in the financial industry. Financial institutions are subject to a wide range of regulations that mandate specific security measures and reporting requirements. Cybersecurity professionals must ensure that the organization complies with these regulations and stays informed about changes in the regulatory landscape.

One of the most significant regulatory frameworks is the General Data Protection Regulation (GDPR), which applies to organizations that process the personal data of EU residents. GDPR imposes strict requirements on data protection and breach notification, and non-compliance can result in significant fines. Cybersecurity professionals must ensure that the organization has robust data protection measures in place and can respond quickly to any data breaches.

In the United States, the New York Department of Financial Services (NYDFS) cybersecurity regulations require financial institutions to establish and maintain comprehensive cybersecurity programs. These regulations include requirements for risk assessments, incident response plans, and periodic testing of security measures. Compliance with these regulations is essential for avoiding legal and financial penalties.

In addition to regulatory compliance, financial institutions must also adhere to industry standards and best practices. Frameworks such as the National Institute of Standards and Technology (NIST) Cybersecurity Framework and the International Organization for Standardization (ISO) 27001 provide guidelines for implementing effective cybersecurity measures. Cybersecurity professionals should use these frameworks to guide their security strategies and ensure that the organization follows best practices.

The role of cybersecurity professionals in the financial industry is increasingly recognized as critical to the overall success and resilience of financial institutions. As cyber threats continue to evolve, the demand for skilled cybersecurity professionals will only grow. Young people interested in pursuing a career in cybersecurity can benefit from a range of educational and professional development opportunities.

Universities and colleges offer degree programs in cybersecurity, information technology, and related fields. These programs provide a strong foundation in technical skills, as well as an understanding of the broader context of cybersecurity in the financial industry. Students can also take advantage of internships and cooperative education programs to gain practical experience and build their professional networks.

Professional organizations such as the Information Systems Security Association (ISSA) and the International Information System Security Certification Consortium (ISC)[2] offer certifications, training programs, and networking opportunities for cybersecurity professionals. These organizations provide valuable resources for continuous learning and professional development.

Online platforms such as Coursera, edX, and Udacity offer a wide range of courses and certifications in cybersecurity. These platforms provide flexible learning options for individuals at all stages of their careers. Whether they are just starting or looking to advance their skills, young professionals can find courses that meet their needs.

For those already working in the financial industry, continuous professional development is essential. Cybersecurity professionals should stay informed about the latest trends and developments in the field, including emerging technologies, new threats, and changes in regulatory requirements. This can be achieved through ongoing training, attending industry conferences, and participating in professional organizations.

In conclusion, cybersecurity is a critical component of the financial industry, essential for protecting sensitive data, maintaining trust, and ensuring stability. As the financial industry becomes increasingly digital, the importance of robust cybersecurity measures will continue to grow. Financial institutions must implement comprehensive security strategies, prioritize incident response and recovery, and build resilience to cyber threats. Regulatory frameworks and collaboration within the industry play a crucial role in enhancing cybersecurity. For young people, developing cybersecurity skills can provide valuable career opportunities and contribute to the development of a more secure and resilient financial system. By staying informed about emerging technologies and best practices, young professionals can help address the evolving cybersecurity challenges facing the financial industry.

12

Algorithmic Trading and Hedge Funds

The world of finance is continually evolving, with technology playing an increasingly pivotal role in shaping the landscape. Two of the most significant developments in modern finance are algorithmic trading and hedge funds. Both have revolutionized how financial markets operate, offering new opportunities and challenges. This chapter delves into the intricacies of algorithmic trading, the structure and strategies of hedge funds, the impact of technology on trading practices, regulatory considerations, ethical dilemmas, and career opportunities in these dynamic fields.

Algorithmic trading, also known as algo trading, involves using computer algorithms to execute trades based on predefined criteria. These algorithms can analyze vast amounts of data, identify trading opportunities, and execute trades at speeds and frequencies that are impossible for human traders. The primary advantage of algorithmic trading is its ability to execute complex trading strategies with precision and efficiency. By automating the trading process, algorithms can react to market conditions in real-time, reducing the likelihood of human error and emotional decision-making.

The origins of algorithmic trading can be traced back to the 1970s when financial institutions began using computers to manage and execute trades. However, it wasn't until the late 1990s and early 2000s, with the advent of high-frequency trading (HFT), that algorithmic trading truly took off. HFT involves using sophisticated algorithms to execute a large number of trades at incredibly high speeds, often in milliseconds. HFT firms leverage their speed advantage to capitalize on small price discrepancies in the market, earning profits through rapid and frequent trading.

One of the key components of algorithmic trading is the use of quantitative models to develop trading strategies. Quantitative analysts, or "quants," use mathematical and statistical techniques to analyze historical market data and identify patterns that can be exploited for profit. These models can range from simple moving averages to complex machine learning algorithms that continuously learn and adapt to changing market conditions.

The strategies employed in algorithmic trading are diverse and can be broadly categorized into several types. One common strategy is market-making, where algorithms place buy and sell orders for a particular asset to provide liquidity to the market. Market makers earn profits through the bid-ask spread, the difference between the buying and selling price of an asset. Another popular strategy is arbitrage, which involves exploiting price discrepancies between different markets or instruments. For example, an algorithm might simultaneously buy an asset in one market where it is undervalued and sell it in another market where it is overvalued, capturing the price difference as profit.

Trend-following is another widely used algorithmic trading strategy. Trend-following algorithms identify and capitalize on trends in the market, such as upward or downward price movements. These algorithms typically use technical indicators, such as moving averages or momentum oscillators, to determine the direction of the trend and execute trades accordingly. Mean reversion is a contrasting strategy that assumes prices will revert to their historical average over time. Algorithms employing mean reversion strategies identify assets that are overbought or oversold and trade them based on the expectation that prices will return to their mean.

Algorithmic trading also encompasses more advanced strategies, such as statistical arbitrage and machine learning-based approaches. Statistical arbitrage involves using statistical models to identify and exploit short-term price inefficiencies between related assets. Machine learning algorithms, on the other hand, leverage vast amounts of data to train predictive models that can anticipate market movements and optimize trading strategies.

While algorithmic trading offers numerous benefits, it also presents several challenges and risks. One of the primary risks is the potential for market manipulation. High-frequency traders, in particular, have been criticized for engaging in practices such as spoofing, where they place large orders with the intention of canceling them to create a false impression of market demand. This can distort prices and undermine market integrity. Additionally, the speed and complexity of algorithmic trading can exacerbate market volatility. Flash crashes, such as the one that occurred on May 6, 2010, when the Dow Jones Industrial Average plummeted nearly 1,000 points in minutes, highlight the potential dangers of algorithmic trading. These incidents often result from feedback loops and algorithmic interactions that cause rapid and unintended price movements.

Regulatory bodies around the world have implemented measures to address the risks associated with algorithmic trading. In the United States, the Securities and Exchange Commission (SEC) and the Commodity Futures Trading Commission (CFTC) have introduced regulations to enhance market transparency and stability. For example, the SEC's Regulation National Market System (Reg NMS) aims to ensure fair and efficient trading by promoting competition and improving price transparency. Similarly, the European Union's Markets in Financial Instruments Directive II (MiFID II) includes provisions to regulate high-frequency trading, requiring firms to have robust risk controls and transparency measures in place.

Hedge funds, another key player in modern finance, are private investment funds that employ a wide range of strategies to generate high returns for their investors. Unlike traditional investment funds, hedge funds have more flexibility in their investment choices and strategies. They can invest in a variety of assets, including stocks, bonds, commodities, currencies, and derivatives. Hedge funds also have the ability to use leverage, or borrowed funds, to amplify their returns.

The structure of hedge funds typically includes a fund manager, who makes investment decisions, and investors, who provide the capital. Hedge fund managers are often compensated through a combination of management fees, based on the total assets under management, and performance fees, based on the fund's profits. This compensation structure aligns the interests of the fund manager with those of the investors, incentivizing the manager to achieve high returns.

Hedge funds employ a wide range of investment strategies, each with its own risk and return profile. Some of the most common strategies include:

Long/Short Equity: This strategy involves taking long positions in undervalued stocks and short positions in overvalued stocks. By hedging their bets, hedge funds aim to generate returns regardless of market direction.

Global Macro: This strategy focuses on macroeconomic trends and events, such as interest rate changes, political developments, and economic indicators. Hedge funds using this strategy may invest in a wide range of assets, including currencies, commodities, and bonds, to capitalize on global economic shifts.

Event-Driven: This strategy seeks to profit from corporate events, such as mergers, acquisitions, bankruptcies, and restructurings. Hedge funds may take positions in companies involved in these events, anticipating that the event will lead to price changes.

Quantitative: This strategy relies on mathematical models and algorithms to identify and exploit market inefficiencies. Quantitative hedge funds, or "quant funds," use data-driven approaches to develop and execute trading strategies.

Relative Value: This strategy involves identifying price discrepancies between related securities and taking positions to profit from the convergence of their prices. Examples include fixed-income arbitrage and convertible arbitrage.

Distressed Securities: This strategy focuses on investing in the debt or equity of companies in financial distress. Hedge funds may seek to profit from the potential recovery or restructuring of these companies.

Hedge funds have a reputation for generating high returns, but they also carry significant risks. The use of leverage can amplify losses as well as gains, leading to substantial volatility. Additionally, the complexity of hedge fund strategies can make it challenging for investors to understand the risks involved. The lack of transparency in hedge fund operations has also raised concerns among regulators and investors.

The impact of technology on hedge funds has been profound. Many hedge funds now employ sophisticated algorithms and data analytics to enhance their investment strategies. The use of big data, machine learning, and artificial intelligence allows hedge funds to analyze vast amounts of information and identify patterns that may not be apparent to human analysts. For example, some hedge funds use natural language processing (NLP) to analyze news articles, social media posts, and other text data to gauge market sentiment and inform trading decisions.

High-frequency trading, a subset of algorithmic trading, has also become a key component of many hedge funds' strategies. By executing trades at high speeds, hedge funds can capitalize on short-term price movements and liquidity imbalances. The use of co-location services, where trading servers are placed in close proximity to exchange servers, further enhances the speed and efficiency of high-frequency trading.

While technology has provided hedge funds with powerful tools for generating returns, it has also introduced new risks and challenges. The reliance on complex algorithms and data-driven models can lead to unforeseen consequences if the models fail or behave unexpectedly. The "quant meltdown" of August 2007, where many quantitative hedge funds experienced significant losses due to simultaneous unwinding of similar positions, illustrates the potential risks of model-driven trading.

The role of regulation in the hedge fund industry is evolving. In response to the financial crisis of 2007-2008, regulators have implemented measures to increase transparency and oversight of hedge funds. The Dodd-Frank Wall Street Reform and Consumer Protection Act, enacted in the United States, introduced new reporting requirements for hedge funds and enhanced the oversight of their activities by the SEC. Similarly, the Alternative Investment Fund Managers Directive (AIFMD) in the European Union aims to regulate hedge fund managers and improve investor protection.

Ethical considerations are also crucial in the context of algorithmic trading and hedge funds. The use of algorithms to execute trades raises questions about fairness, market integrity, and the potential for manipulation. High-frequency trading, in particular, has been criticized for creating an uneven playing field, where firms with advanced technology and faster access to market data have a competitive advantage over traditional investors.

To address these ethical concerns, financial institutions and regulators must ensure that trading practices are transparent and fair. This includes implementing measures to prevent market manipulation, ensuring that algorithms operate within ethical guidelines, and promoting transparency in trading activities. Additionally, fostering a culture of ethical behavior within financial institutions is essential for maintaining trust and integrity in the markets.

For young people interested in pursuing a career in algorithmic trading or hedge funds, the opportunities are vast and varied. A strong foundation in mathematics, statistics, computer science, and finance is essential for success in these fields. Developing expertise in programming languages such as Python, R, and C++ can provide a significant advantage, as these languages are commonly used in developing trading algorithms and data analysis.

Educational institutions, professional organizations, and online platforms offer a wide range of resources and courses to help young people develop the necessary skills. Participating in internships and cooperative education programs can provide valuable hands-on experience and networking opportunities. Gaining practical experience through internships at hedge funds, investment banks, or financial technology firms can provide insights into the industry and help build a professional network.

Certifications such as the Chartered Financial Analyst (CFA) designation can also enhance job prospects and provide a strong foundation in investment principles and practices. Additionally, staying informed about the latest developments in technology, financial markets, and regulatory changes is crucial for staying competitive in these dynamic fields.

In conclusion, algorithmic trading and hedge funds represent significant advancements in modern finance, offering new opportunities and challenges. The use of technology, sophisticated algorithms, and quantitative models has revolutionized trading practices and investment strategies. However, these advancements also introduce new risks and ethical considerations that must be carefully managed. For young people, developing the necessary skills and knowledge can open up exciting career opportunities in these dynamic and rapidly evolving fields. By staying informed, continuously learning, and adhering to ethical principles, young professionals can contribute to the growth and innovation of the financial industry.

13

Behavioral Economics in Finance

Behavioral economics is a field that combines insights from psychology and economics to understand how people make financial decisions. Unlike traditional economic theories that assume individuals act rationally and in their best interests, behavioral economics recognizes that people often behave irrationally due to cognitive biases, emotions, and social influences. This chapter explores the key concepts of behavioral economics, common cognitive biases that influence investor behavior, strategies for improving financial decision-making, and the impact of behavioral economics on financial markets and policy.

Behavioral economics emerged as a distinct field in the late 20th century, challenging the traditional assumptions of rationality in economic models. Pioneers like Daniel Kahneman and Amos Tversky conducted groundbreaking research that revealed systematic biases in human decision-making. Their work laid the foundation for understanding how psychological factors influence economic behavior.

One of the central concepts in behavioral economics is bounded rationality. Traditional economic theories assume that individuals have unlimited cognitive resources and access to all relevant information, allowing them to make optimal decisions. In reality, people have limited cognitive abilities and often rely on heuristics, or mental shortcuts, to make decisions. These heuristics can lead to biases and errors in judgment.

Cognitive biases are systematic patterns of deviation from rationality that can affect financial decision-making.

Some of the most common cognitive biases include:

Overconfidence:

- Overconfidence is the tendency to overestimate one's abilities, knowledge, and predictions. In finance, overconfident investors may take excessive risks, trade too frequently, and underestimate the likelihood of negative outcomes. This can lead to significant financial losses and increased market volatility.

Anchoring:

- Anchoring occurs when individuals rely too heavily on the first piece of information they encounter when making decisions. For example, an investor may anchor on the initial price of a stock and fail to adjust their expectations based on new information. This can lead to suboptimal investment decisions and resistance to changing market conditions.

Herd Behavior:

- Herd behavior is the tendency to follow the actions of others, often without independent analysis. In financial markets, herd behavior can lead to asset bubbles and market crashes, as investors buy or sell based on the actions of others rather than fundamental analysis.

Loss Aversion:

- Loss aversion is the tendency to prefer avoiding losses over acquiring equivalent gains. People experience the pain of losses more intensely than the pleasure of gains, leading to risk-averse behavior. In finance, loss aversion can result in holding onto losing investments for too long or selling winning investments prematurely.

Mental Accounting:

- Mental accounting refers to the tendency to categorize and treat money differently based on its source or intended use. For example, an investor might treat a tax refund differently from regular income, leading to different spending or investment decisions. This can result in inefficient financial management and suboptimal investment choices.

Confirmation Bias:

- Confirmation bias is the tendency to seek out and interpret information that confirms one's preexisting beliefs while ignoring or dismissing contradictory information. In finance, confirmation bias can lead to overconfidence in investment decisions and resistance to changing strategies based on new evidence.

Recency Effect:

- The recency effect is the tendency to give greater weight to recent information or events when making decisions. Investors influenced by the recency effect may overreact to short-term market movements and make impulsive trading decisions, leading to increased volatility and potential losses.

Understanding these cognitive biases is crucial for improving financial decision-making. By recognizing and addressing biases, investors can make more rational and informed choices.

Several strategies can help mitigate the impact of cognitive biases on financial decisions:

Education and Awareness:

- Increasing awareness of cognitive biases and their impact on decision-making is the first step toward improving financial behavior. Investors can benefit from educational programs and resources that teach the principles of behavioral economics and the common biases that affect financial decisions.

Diversification:

- Diversifying investments across different asset classes, sectors, and geographic regions can help reduce the impact of individual biases and mitigate risk. A diversified portfolio is less susceptible to the effects of overconfidence, loss aversion, and other biases.

Setting Clear Goals:

- Establishing clear and specific financial goals can help investors stay focused and avoid impulsive decisions. By defining objectives and creating a plan to achieve them, investors can reduce the influence of short-term market fluctuations and cognitive biases.

Automating Decisions:

- Automating certain financial decisions, such as regular contributions to savings or investment accounts, can help reduce the impact of emotional and cognitive biases. Automation ensures consistency and discipline in financial behavior, reducing the likelihood of impulsive or biased decisions.

Seeking Professional Advice:

- Working with a financial advisor can provide an objective perspective and help investors make more informed decisions. Advisors can offer guidance on managing cognitive biases, developing a diversified investment strategy, and staying focused on long-term goals.

Behavioral economics has also had a significant impact on financial markets and policy. Understanding how psychological factors influence investor behavior can help policymakers design more effective regulations and interventions. For example, insights from behavioral economics have led to the development of "nudges," which are subtle changes in the environment that encourage desired behaviors without restricting freedom of choice.

One of the most well-known applications of nudges in finance is automatic enrollment in retirement savings plans. Research has shown that automatically enrolling employees in retirement plans, with the option to opt-out, significantly increases participation rates. This approach leverages inertia and the tendency to stick with the default option to promote better financial outcomes.

Behavioral economics has also informed the design of financial products and services. For example, robo-advisors use algorithms and behavioral insights to provide personalized investment recommendations and help investors stay on track with their goals. By incorporating principles of behavioral economics, robo-advisors can help mitigate biases and improve financial decision-making.

The field of behavioral finance, a sub-discipline of behavioral economics, specifically examines how cognitive biases and emotions influence investment decisions. Behavioral finance researchers study market anomalies and patterns that cannot be explained by traditional economic theories. For example, the January effect, where stock prices tend to rise in January, and the disposition effect, where investors are more likely to sell winning investments and hold onto losers, are phenomena that behavioral finance seeks to understand.

Behavioral finance also explores how investor sentiment and emotions can drive market trends and contribute to asset bubbles and crashes. During periods of market exuberance, positive sentiment can lead to overvaluation of assets, while fear and panic can result in sharp market declines. Understanding these dynamics can help investors and policymakers anticipate and respond to market cycles.

For young people interested in finance, understanding behavioral economics is crucial for making better financial decisions and navigating the complexities of the financial markets. Developing a strong foundation in psychology and economics can provide valuable insights into human behavior and its impact on finance. Courses and certifications in behavioral economics and finance can enhance knowledge and job prospects.

Practical experience is also essential for understanding behavioral economics in finance. Internships, research projects, and involvement in investment clubs can provide hands-on learning opportunities and help young professionals apply behavioral insights to real-world financial decisions. Engaging with industry professionals and participating in conferences and seminars can further deepen understanding and build a professional network.

Behavioral economics also emphasizes the importance of continuous learning and self-awareness. Investors should regularly evaluate their financial behavior, reflect on past decisions, and identify areas for improvement. By staying informed about the latest research and developments in behavioral economics, investors can continually refine their strategies and make more rational choices.

Ethical considerations are an important aspect of behavioral economics in finance. Financial professionals must ensure that their use of behavioral insights and nudges is aligned with the best interests of their clients. Transparency, fairness, and respect for autonomy are essential principles that should guide the application of behavioral economics in financial services.

In conclusion, behavioral economics provides a valuable framework for understanding how cognitive biases, emotions, and social influences shape financial decisions. By recognizing and addressing these biases, investors can make more rational and informed choices, leading to better financial outcomes. Behavioral economics also has significant implications for financial markets and policy, informing the design of regulations, products, and interventions that promote better financial behavior. For young people, developing expertise in behavioral economics can enhance career opportunities and contribute to more effective and ethical financial decision-making. By staying informed, continuously learning, and applying behavioral insights, young professionals can navigate the complexities of the financial markets and achieve their financial goals.

14

Emerging Trends in Payments

The landscape of payments is rapidly evolving, driven by technological advancements and changing consumer behaviors. Traditional payment methods, such as cash and checks, are increasingly being replaced by digital solutions that offer greater convenience, security, and efficiency. This chapter explores the evolution of payment systems, the rise of digital payment solutions, the impact of contactless payments and digital wallets, the role of cryptocurrency payments, and the challenges and opportunities associated with these emerging trends.

The evolution of payment systems has been marked by several key milestones, each bringing significant improvements in how transactions are conducted. In the early days of commerce, bartering was the primary means of exchange, where goods and services were traded directly. The introduction of money, in the form of coins and later banknotes, revolutionized trade by providing a standardized medium of exchange.

The development of banking systems and financial institutions further transformed payments, enabling the creation of checks, credit cards, and electronic funds transfers. These innovations made it possible to conduct transactions without physical cash, paving the way for the digital payment solutions we see today.

One of the most significant trends in the payments industry is the rise of digital payment solutions. Digital payments encompass a wide range of technologies and platforms that facilitate the transfer of money electronically. This includes online banking, mobile banking, digital wallets, and payment apps.

Digital wallets, such as Apple Pay, Google Pay, and Samsung Pay, have gained widespread adoption, allowing users to store their payment information securely on their smartphones and make payments with a simple tap or scan. These wallets use near-field communication (NFC) technology to enable contactless payments, making transactions quick and convenient.

Mobile payment apps, such as PayPal, Venmo, and Cash App, have also become popular, enabling peer-to-peer (P2P) transfers and online purchases. These apps offer features like instant transfers, bill splitting, and payment requests, making them versatile tools for managing personal finances.

The adoption of digital payment solutions has been accelerated by several factors, including the proliferation of smartphones, the growth of e-commerce, and the increasing demand for convenience and security. Consumers are increasingly comfortable with using digital platforms for their financial transactions, and businesses are responding by integrating these solutions into their payment systems.

Contactless payments, in particular, have seen significant growth in recent years. Contactless payment methods allow users to make transactions by simply tapping their card or mobile device on a payment terminal equipped with NFC technology. This method offers several advantages over traditional payment methods, including speed, convenience, and hygiene.

One of the key drivers of contactless payments is the growing adoption of NFC-enabled devices. Most modern smartphones come equipped with NFC technology, allowing users to link their credit or debit cards to their mobile wallets and make contactless payments. Additionally, many credit and debit cards now come with built-in NFC chips, enabling contactless transactions at point-of-sale terminals.

The COVID-19 pandemic further accelerated the adoption of contactless payments as consumers and businesses sought to minimize physical contact and reduce the risk of virus transmission. Many retailers and service providers encouraged the use of contactless payments, and some even implemented contactless-only policies to enhance safety.

The rise of digital wallets and contactless payments has also had a significant impact on financial inclusion. Digital payment solutions provide a convenient and accessible way for individuals to participate in the financial system, particularly in regions where traditional banking infrastructure is lacking. For example, mobile money platforms like M-Pesa in Kenya have revolutionized financial inclusion by allowing users to store and transfer money using their mobile phones.

Cryptocurrency payments represent another emerging trend in the payments landscape. Cryptocurrencies, such as Bitcoin, Ethereum, and Litecoin, offer an alternative to traditional fiat currencies and enable peer-to-peer transactions without the need for intermediaries like banks. Cryptocurrency payments are facilitated by blockchain technology, which provides a secure and transparent way to record and verify transactions.

One of the main advantages of cryptocurrency payments is their potential for lower transaction fees compared to traditional payment methods. Because cryptocurrencies operate on decentralized networks, they eliminate the need for intermediaries, reducing the costs associated with processing payments. This can be particularly beneficial for cross-border transactions, where traditional payment methods often involve high fees and lengthy processing times.

Cryptocurrency payments also offer enhanced security and privacy. Transactions are recorded on a public blockchain, making them transparent and tamper-proof. Additionally, users can make transactions without revealing their personal information, protecting their privacy.

However, there are several challenges associated with cryptocurrency payments that need to be addressed before they can achieve mainstream adoption. One of the primary challenges is the volatility of cryptocurrency prices. The value of cryptocurrencies can fluctuate significantly, making them less stable and reliable as a medium of exchange. This volatility can create uncertainty for both consumers and merchants, making it difficult to price goods and services in cryptocurrency.

Regulatory uncertainty is another significant challenge for cryptocurrency payments. Governments and regulatory bodies around the world are still grappling with how to classify and regulate cryptocurrencies. The lack of clear and consistent regulations creates risks for users and businesses, as they may face legal and compliance issues. For example, some countries have banned or restricted the use of cryptocurrencies, while others have introduced regulations to ensure transparency and prevent illegal activities.

Security concerns are also a critical issue for cryptocurrency payments. While blockchain technology provides a secure framework for transactions, the digital wallets and exchanges used to store and trade cryptocurrencies can be vulnerable to hacking and theft. High-profile incidents, such as the Mt. Gox hack in 2014, where approximately 850,000 Bitcoins were stolen, highlight the risks associated with cryptocurrency security. Ensuring the security of cryptocurrency transactions and storage remains a top priority for the industry.

Despite these challenges, the adoption of cryptocurrency payments is growing, and several companies are beginning to accept cryptocurrencies as a form of payment. For example, major companies like Tesla, Microsoft, and Overstock have announced that they will accept Bitcoin for purchases. Additionally, payment processors like PayPal and Square have integrated cryptocurrency services, allowing users to buy, sell, and hold cryptocurrencies within their platforms.

The integration of cryptocurrency payments into mainstream financial systems also opens up new possibilities for innovation and financial inclusion. For example, decentralized finance (DeFi) platforms leverage blockchain technology to offer a range of financial services, including lending, borrowing, and trading, without the need for traditional intermediaries. DeFi platforms can provide access to financial services for individuals who are underserved by traditional banking systems, enhancing financial inclusion and empowerment.

As digital payment solutions continue to evolve, several trends and innovations are shaping the future of payments. One of the most significant trends is the use of biometric authentication for payments. Biometric authentication, such as fingerprint recognition, facial recognition, and voice recognition, offers a secure and convenient way to verify user identities and authorize transactions. Many smartphones and payment apps now support biometric authentication, enhancing security and user experience.

Another emerging trend is the use of artificial intelligence (AI) and machine learning in payment systems. AI can enhance fraud detection and prevention by analyzing transaction patterns and identifying suspicious activities in real-time. Machine learning algorithms can continuously learn and adapt to new threats, improving the accuracy and effectiveness of fraud detection systems. AI can also enhance customer service by providing personalized recommendations and support through chatbots and virtual assistants.

The Internet of Things (IoT) is also transforming the payments landscape by enabling connected devices to facilitate transactions. IoT devices, such as smartwatches, fitness trackers, and home assistants, can be integrated with payment systems, allowing users to make payments seamlessly through their devices. For example, a smartwatch with an NFC chip can be used to make contactless payments, while a smart refrigerator can automatically reorder groceries and make payments on behalf of the user.

Tokenization is another innovation that is enhancing the security of digital payments. Tokenization involves replacing sensitive payment information, such as credit card numbers, with unique tokens that can be used for transactions. These tokens are meaningless to hackers, reducing the risk of data breaches and fraud. Tokenization is widely used in mobile wallets and payment apps to protect user information and ensure secure transactions.

The rise of central bank digital currencies (CBDCs) represents a significant development in the payments landscape. CBDCs are digital versions of a country's national currency, issued and regulated by the central bank. Unlike cryptocurrencies, which operate on decentralized networks, CBDCs are centralized and backed by the government. CBDCs offer several benefits, including faster and cheaper transactions, enhanced financial inclusion, and improved monetary policy implementation.

Several countries, including China, Sweden, and the Bahamas, have already launched or are in the process of developing their own CBDCs. The People's Bank of China (PBOC) has been at the forefront of CBDC development, launching a pilot program for its digital currency, the Digital Currency Electronic Payment (DCEP), in several cities. The introduction of CBDCs has the potential to reshape the payments landscape, offering a secure and efficient alternative to traditional payment methods.

The future of payments is also likely to be shaped by the concept of open banking. Open banking involves the sharing of financial data between banks and third-party service providers through secure APIs (Application Programming Interfaces). This enables the development of innovative financial services and products that can provide greater value to consumers.

For example, third-party apps can aggregate information from multiple bank accounts, provide personalized financial insights, and offer tailored financial products. Open banking has the potential to enhance competition, innovation, and consumer choice in the financial services industry.

Despite the exciting developments and opportunities in the payments landscape, several challenges remain. Security and privacy concerns are paramount, as the digital nature of payments makes them susceptible to cyberattacks and data breaches. Ensuring the security of payment systems and protecting user information are critical priorities for the industry.

Regulatory and legal issues also present challenges for the adoption and implementation of new payment technologies. Clear and consistent regulations are needed to provide a stable and secure environment for digital payments. Additionally, addressing the digital divide and ensuring that all individuals have access to digital payment solutions is essential for promoting financial inclusion.

For young people interested in pursuing a career in finance, understanding the emerging trends in payments is crucial. The demand for professionals with expertise in digital payments, cybersecurity, and financial technology is growing, and developing skills in these areas can open up exciting career opportunities.

Educational institutions, professional organizations, and online platforms offer a wide range of resources and courses to help young people develop the necessary skills. Certifications such as Certified Payments Professional (CPP) and Certified Treasury Professional (CTP) can provide valuable credentials and enhance job prospects. Gaining practical experience through internships and involvement in fintech initiatives can also provide hands-on learning and networking opportunities.

In conclusion, the payments landscape is undergoing a profound transformation, driven by technological advancements and changing consumer behaviors. The rise of digital payment solutions, contactless payments, digital wallets, and cryptocurrency payments is reshaping how transactions are conducted. Emerging trends such as biometric authentication, AI, IoT, tokenization, and CBDCs offer exciting possibilities for the future of payments. For young people, understanding these trends and developing relevant skills can provide valuable career opportunities and contribute to the development of a more secure, efficient, and inclusive financial system. By staying informed and embracing innovation, young professionals can navigate the evolving payments landscape and make a meaningful impact on the future of finance.

15

Risk Management in the Digital Era

The digital era has brought significant advancements in technology and innovation, transforming the financial industry. However, with these advancements come new risks and challenges that financial institutions must address to ensure stability, security, and trust. Risk management in the digital era involves identifying, assessing, and mitigating various financial risks, including cybersecurity threats, regulatory compliance, and operational risks. This chapter explores the importance of risk management in the digital era, strategies for mitigating fintech risks, the role of regulatory compliance, and the development of resilient financial systems.

Risk management is a critical aspect of the financial industry, essential for protecting assets, maintaining stability, and ensuring regulatory compliance. In the digital era, the complexity and interconnectedness of financial systems have increased, introducing new risks that must be managed effectively. Financial institutions must adopt a proactive and comprehensive approach to risk management to navigate the evolving landscape and protect their operations.

One of the primary risks in the digital era is cybersecurity. Cyber threats are becoming more sophisticated and prevalent, targeting financial institutions to steal sensitive data, disrupt operations, and perpetrate fraud. Cyberattacks can have severe consequences, including financial losses, reputational damage, and regulatory penalties. To mitigate cybersecurity risks, financial institutions must implement robust security measures, including encryption, multi-factor authentication, and intrusion detection systems.

Encryption is a fundamental security measure that protects sensitive data by converting it into unreadable code. This ensures that even if data is intercepted, it cannot be accessed or deciphered without the encryption key. Multi-factor authentication (MFA) adds an extra layer of security by requiring users to provide multiple forms of identification, such as a password and a one-time code sent to their mobile device. MFA makes it more challenging for cybercriminals to gain unauthorized access to accounts.

Intrusion detection systems (IDS) are essential for monitoring network traffic and identifying suspicious activities. IDS can detect and alert security teams to potential threats, allowing them to respond quickly and mitigate risks. Regular security assessments and penetration testing are also crucial for identifying vulnerabilities and ensuring that security measures are up to date.

Employee training and awareness are vital components of a robust cybersecurity strategy. Human error is often a significant factor in security breaches, with employees inadvertently clicking on malicious links or falling victim to phishing scams. Regular training programs can educate employees about cybersecurity best practices, how to recognize and respond to potential threats, and the importance of maintaining a security-conscious mindset.

Incident response and recovery are critical aspects of cybersecurity in finance. Despite the best efforts to prevent cyberattacks, incidents can still occur. Having a well-defined incident response plan is essential for minimizing the impact of a cyberattack and ensuring a swift recovery. An effective incident response plan should include clear procedures for detecting and reporting incidents, roles and responsibilities for the response team, and steps for containing and mitigating the attack.

One of the first steps in incident response is to identify the scope and nature of the attack. This involves analyzing logs, network traffic, and other indicators to determine how the attack occurred, what systems and data were affected, and the extent of the damage. Once the scope of the attack is understood, the next step is to contain it to prevent further damage. This may involve isolating affected systems, blocking malicious IP addresses, and disabling compromised accounts.

After containing the attack, the focus shifts to eradicating the threat. This involves removing malware, patching vulnerabilities, and restoring affected systems from backups. Ensuring that all traces of the attack are eliminated is crucial to prevent a recurrence. Once the threat is eradicated, the recovery phase begins, which involves restoring normal operations and addressing any residual impacts.

Communication is a critical component of incident response. Financial institutions must communicate with affected customers, regulators, and other stakeholders to inform them about the incident and the steps being taken to address it. Transparency and timely communication can help maintain trust and mitigate the reputational damage associated with a cyberattack.

In addition to incident response, financial institutions must also focus on building resilience to cyber threats. This involves implementing measures to ensure that critical systems and data can continue to operate even in the face of an attack. Business continuity planning and disaster recovery are key components of building resilience. These plans should outline procedures for maintaining operations and recovering from disruptions, including cyberattacks.

Business continuity planning involves identifying critical business functions, assessing potential risks, and developing strategies to ensure that these functions can continue during and after a disruption. This may include establishing backup systems, creating redundancy in critical processes, and developing communication plans to keep stakeholders informed.

Disaster recovery focuses on restoring IT systems and data after a disruption. This involves creating backup copies of data, implementing failover systems to switch to backup servers, and developing procedures for restoring normal operations. Regular testing of disaster recovery plans is essential to ensure that they are effective and can be executed smoothly in the event of a disruption.

Cyber insurance is another tool that financial institutions can use to mitigate the financial impact of cyber incidents. Cyber insurance policies can provide coverage for various costs associated with a cyber incident, such as legal fees, notification costs, and business interruption losses. However, it is essential to carefully review and understand the terms and conditions of the policy to ensure that it provides adequate coverage for the specific risks faced by the institution.

The role of risk culture in financial institutions is also crucial for effective risk management. A strong risk culture involves fostering an environment where employees are aware of risks, understand their responsibilities in managing risks, and are encouraged to report potential issues. Leadership plays a key role in setting the tone for risk culture, promoting transparency, accountability, and continuous improvement.

Training and awareness programs are essential for building a strong risk culture. Employees should receive regular training on risk management practices, cybersecurity awareness, and regulatory compliance. This helps ensure that they understand the risks facing the institution and their role in mitigating these risks. Encouraging open communication and providing channels for reporting potential issues can also help identify and address risks before they escalate.

Collaboration and information sharing are critical for enhancing risk management in the financial industry. Financial institutions should collaborate with industry peers, government agencies, and cybersecurity organizations to share information about threats, vulnerabilities, and best practices. Initiatives such as the Financial Services Information Sharing and Analysis Center (FS-ISAC) provide a platform for information sharing and collaboration within the financial sector.

Emerging technologies, such as artificial intelligence (AI) and machine learning (ML), offer new opportunities for enhancing risk management in finance. AI and ML can analyze vast amounts of data in real-time to detect and respond to risks more quickly and accurately. For example, AI-driven risk management systems can identify unusual patterns of behavior that may indicate fraud or other suspicious activities and automatically initiate response measures. Similarly, ML algorithms can continuously learn and adapt to new threats, improving their effectiveness over time.

Blockchain technology also holds promise for enhancing risk management in finance. The decentralized and immutable nature of blockchain can provide a secure and transparent way to record and verify transactions, reducing the risk of fraud and tampering. Blockchain can be used to enhance the security of various financial processes, such as identity verification, transaction settlement, and supply chain management.

Despite the potential benefits, the adoption of emerging technologies also introduces new risks and challenges. For example, AI and ML systems can be vulnerable to adversarial attacks, where malicious actors manipulate the input data to deceive the algorithms. Similarly, the complexity of blockchain technology can create new attack vectors that need to be addressed. Financial institutions must carefully evaluate the risks and benefits of emerging technologies and implement appropriate security measures to mitigate these risks.

Operational risk is another significant concern in the digital era. Operational risk refers to the potential for losses resulting from inadequate or failed internal processes, systems, or human errors. The complexity of digital financial systems increases the likelihood of operational failures, making it essential for financial institutions to implement robust risk management frameworks.

One effective strategy for managing operational risk is the implementation of governance, risk, and compliance (GRC) frameworks. GRC frameworks provide a structured approach to managing regulatory requirements, risks, and controls. They involve identifying and assessing risks, implementing policies and procedures to mitigate risks, and continuously monitoring and reporting on risk management activities.

Technology can play a critical role in supporting GRC efforts. Regtech, short for regulatory technology, refers to the use of technology to enhance regulatory compliance and risk management. Regtech solutions can automate compliance processes, such as transaction monitoring, reporting, and risk assessments, reducing the administrative burden and improving the accuracy and efficiency of compliance activities. For example, AI-driven regtech solutions can analyze large volumes of transaction data in real-time to detect suspicious activities and generate automated reports for regulatory authorities.

Building resilience in financial systems is crucial for mitigating risks and ensuring stability. Resilience involves the ability to withstand and recover from disruptions, such as cyberattacks, natural disasters, and operational failures. Business continuity planning and disaster recovery are key components of building resilience. These plans should outline procedures for maintaining operations and recovering from disruptions, including cyberattacks.

Business continuity planning involves identifying critical business functions, assessing potential risks, and developing strategies to ensure that these functions can continue during and after a disruption. This may include establishing backup systems, creating redundancy in critical processes, and developing communication plans to keep stakeholders informed.

Disaster recovery focuses on restoring IT systems and data after a disruption. This involves creating backup copies of data, implementing failover systems to switch to backup servers, and developing procedures for restoring normal operations. Regular testing of disaster recovery plans is essential to ensure that they are effective and can be executed smoothly in the event of a disruption.

Cyber insurance is another tool that financial institutions can use to mitigate the financial impact of cyber incidents. Cyber insurance policies can provide coverage for various costs associated with a cyber incident, such as legal fees, notification costs, and business interruption losses. However, it is essential to carefully review and understand the terms and conditions of the policy to ensure that it provides adequate coverage for the specific risks faced by the institution.

The role of risk culture in financial institutions is also crucial for effective risk management. A strong risk culture involves fostering an environment where employees are aware of risks, understand their responsibilities in managing risks, and are encouraged to report potential issues. Leadership plays a key role in setting the tone for risk culture, promoting transparency, accountability, and continuous improvement.

Training and awareness programs are essential for building a strong risk culture. Employees should receive regular training on risk management practices, cybersecurity awareness, and regulatory compliance. This helps ensure that they understand the risks facing the institution and their role in mitigating these risks. Encouraging open communication and providing channels for reporting potential issues can also help identify and address risks before they escalate.

Collaboration and information sharing are critical for enhancing risk management in the financial industry. Financial institutions should collaborate with industry peers, government agencies, and cybersecurity organizations to share information about threats, vulnerabilities, and best practices. Initiatives such as the Financial Services Information Sharing and Analysis Center (FS-ISAC) provide a platform for information sharing and collaboration within the financial sector.

Emerging technologies, such as artificial intelligence (AI) and machine learning (ML), offer new opportunities for enhancing risk management in finance. AI and ML can analyze vast amounts of data in real-time to detect and respond to risks more quickly and accurately. For example, AI-driven risk management systems can identify unusual patterns of behavior that may indicate fraud or other suspicious activities and automatically initiate response measures. Similarly, ML algorithms can continuously learn and adapt to new threats, improving their effectiveness over time.

Blockchain technology also holds promise for enhancing risk management in finance. The decentralized and immutable nature of blockchain can provide a secure and transparent way to record and verify transactions, reducing the risk of fraud and tampering. Blockchain can be used to enhance the security of various financial processes, such as identity verification, transaction settlement, and supply chain management.

Despite the potential benefits, the adoption of emerging technologies also introduces new risks and challenges. For example, AI and ML systems can be vulnerable to adversarial attacks, where malicious actors manipulate the input data to deceive the algorithms. Similarly, the complexity of blockchain technology can create new attack vectors that need to be addressed. Financial institutions must carefully evaluate the risks and benefits of emerging technologies and implement appropriate security measures to mitigate these risks.

For young people interested in pursuing a career in finance, understanding risk management is crucial. The demand for professionals with expertise in risk management, cybersecurity, and regulatory compliance is growing, and developing skills in these areas can open up exciting career opportunities. Key skills for risk management professionals include knowledge of risk assessment, cybersecurity, regulatory compliance, and business continuity planning. Additionally, staying informed about the latest trends and developments in risk management is crucial for staying ahead of emerging threats.

Educational institutions, professional organizations, and online platforms offer a wide range of resources and courses to help young people develop the necessary skills. Certifications such as the Certified Risk Manager (CRM) and the Certified Information Systems Auditor (CISA) can provide valuable credentials and enhance job prospects. Gaining practical experience through internships and involvement in risk management initiatives can also provide hands-on learning and networking opportunities.

In conclusion, risk management in the digital era is essential for protecting assets, maintaining stability, and ensuring regulatory compliance in the financial industry. Financial institutions must adopt a proactive and comprehensive approach to risk management to navigate the evolving landscape and protect their operations. This involves implementing robust security measures, adhering to regulatory requirements, and building resilience to withstand and recover from disruptions. Emerging technologies, such as AI, ML, and blockchain, offer new opportunities for enhancing risk management but also introduce new risks that must be carefully managed. For young people, developing expertise in risk management can provide valuable career opportunities and contribute to the development of a more secure and resilient financial system. By staying informed and embracing innovation, young professionals can navigate the complexities of risk management in the digital era and make a meaningful impact on the future of finance.

Furthermore, the importance of fostering a strong risk culture within financial institutions cannot be overstated. Encouraging a culture where employees are aware of the risks, understand their responsibilities, and feel empowered to report potential issues is crucial. Leadership plays a key role in setting the tone for risk culture by promoting transparency, accountability, and continuous improvement.

Collaboration and information sharing are critical for enhancing risk management in the financial industry. Financial institutions should collaborate with industry peers, government agencies, and cybersecurity organizations to share information about threats, vulnerabilities, and best practices. Initiatives such as the Financial Services Information Sharing and Analysis Center (FS-ISAC) provide a platform for information sharing and collaboration within the financial sector.

Emerging technologies, such as artificial intelligence (AI) and machine learning (ML), offer new opportunities for enhancing risk management in finance. AI and ML can analyze vast amounts of data in real-time to detect and respond to risks more quickly and accurately. For example, AI-driven risk management systems can identify unusual patterns of behavior that may indicate fraud or other suspicious activities and automatically initiate response measures. Similarly, ML algorithms can continuously learn and adapt to new threats, improving their effectiveness over time.

Blockchain technology also holds promise for enhancing risk management in finance. The decentralized and immutable nature of blockchain can provide a secure and transparent way to record and verify transactions, reducing the risk of fraud and tampering. Blockchain can be used to enhance the security of various financial processes, such as identity verification, transaction settlement, and supply chain management.

Despite the potential benefits, the adoption of emerging technologies also introduces new risks and challenges. For example, AI and ML systems can be vulnerable to adversarial attacks, where malicious actors manipulate the input data to deceive the algorithms. Similarly, the complexity of blockchain technology can create new attack vectors that need to be addressed. Financial institutions must carefully evaluate the risks and benefits of emerging technologies and implement appropriate security measures to mitigate these risks.

For young people interested in pursuing a career in finance, understanding risk management is crucial. The demand for professionals with expertise in risk management, cybersecurity, and regulatory compliance is growing, and developing skills in these areas can open up exciting career opportunities. Key skills for risk management professionals include knowledge of risk assessment, cybersecurity, regulatory compliance, and business continuity planning. Additionally, staying informed about the latest trends and developments in risk management is crucial for staying ahead of emerging threats.

Educational institutions, professional organizations, and online platforms offer a wide range of resources and courses to help young people develop the necessary skills. Certifications such as the Certified Risk Manager (CRM) and the Certified Information Systems Auditor (CISA) can provide valuable credentials and enhance job prospects. Gaining practical experience through internships and involvement in risk management initiatives can also provide hands-on learning and networking opportunities.

In conclusion, risk management in the digital era is essential for protecting assets, maintaining stability, and ensuring regulatory compliance in the financial industry. Financial institutions must adopt a proactive and comprehensive approach to risk management to navigate the evolving landscape and protect their operations. This involves implementing robust security measures, adhering to regulatory requirements, and building resilience to withstand and recover from disruptions. Emerging technologies, such as AI, ML, and blockchain, offer new opportunities for enhancing risk management but also introduce new risks that must be carefully managed. For young people, developing expertise in risk management can provide valuable career opportunities and contribute to the development of a more secure and resilient financial system. By staying informed and embracing innovation, young professionals can navigate the complexities of risk management in the digital era and make a meaningful impact on the future of finance.

16

Navigating Career Paths in Finance and Technology

The convergence of finance and technology, often referred to as fintech, has created a dynamic and rapidly evolving industry. This sector offers a wide range of career opportunities that combine financial expertise with technological skills. As fintech continues to transform traditional financial services, there is a growing demand for professionals who can navigate this landscape and drive innovation. This chapter explores various career paths in finance and technology, the skills required for success, and strategies for building a rewarding career in this exciting field.

The rise of fintech has disrupted traditional financial services by introducing innovative solutions for payments, lending, investing, and more. This disruption has created new job roles and opportunities across the financial sector. Some of the most prominent areas within fintech include digital banking, blockchain, artificial intelligence (AI) and machine learning (ML), cybersecurity, and regulatory technology (regtech).

Digital banking has revolutionized the way individuals and businesses manage their finances. Online-only banks, also known as neobanks or challenger banks, offer services such as checking and savings accounts, loans, and investment products without the need for physical branches. These banks leverage technology to provide seamless and user-friendly experiences, attracting a growing number of customers. Careers in digital banking encompass a wide range of roles, including software development, product management, user experience (UX) design, and data analysis. Professionals in this field work to create and enhance digital banking platforms, ensuring they meet customer needs and comply with regulatory requirements. Key skills for success in digital banking include proficiency in programming languages, an understanding of financial products, and strong problem-solving abilities.

Blockchain technology, which underpins cryptocurrencies like Bitcoin and Ethereum, has the potential to transform various aspects of finance, from payments to supply chain management. Careers in blockchain and cryptocurrency involve developing and maintaining blockchain networks, creating decentralized applications (dApps), and managing cryptocurrency exchanges. Key roles in this field include blockchain developers, cryptographers, and blockchain project managers. Blockchain developers design and implement blockchain protocols and smart contracts, while cryptographers focus on securing blockchain networks. Blockchain project managers oversee the development and implementation of blockchain projects, ensuring they meet business objectives and regulatory standards. To succeed in blockchain and cryptocurrency careers, professionals need a strong foundation in computer science, cryptography, and distributed systems. Additionally, staying informed about the latest developments in blockchain technology and regulatory changes is crucial for navigating this rapidly evolving field.

AI and ML are transforming finance by enabling more efficient and accurate decision-making. These technologies are used for a variety of applications, including algorithmic trading, fraud detection, credit scoring, and customer service. Careers in AI and ML involve developing and deploying algorithms that can analyze vast amounts of data and generate insights. Key roles in this field include data scientists, machine learning engineers, and AI researchers. Data scientists analyze financial data to identify trends and patterns, while machine learning engineers develop and implement ML models. AI researchers focus on advancing the field of AI by exploring new algorithms and techniques. To build a career in AI and ML, professionals need strong skills in mathematics, statistics, and programming. Proficiency in languages such as Python and R, as well as experience with ML frameworks like TensorFlow and PyTorch, is essential. Additionally, a solid understanding of financial markets and products can enhance the application of AI and ML in finance.

As financial institutions become increasingly digital, cybersecurity has become a critical concern. Cybersecurity professionals work to protect financial systems and data from cyber threats, ensuring the security and integrity of financial transactions. Careers in cybersecurity involve developing and implementing security measures, monitoring for potential threats, and responding to security incidents. Key roles in this field include cybersecurity analysts, ethical hackers, and security architects. Cybersecurity analysts monitor networks for suspicious activity and investigate security breaches. Ethical hackers, also known as penetration testers, simulate cyberattacks to identify vulnerabilities in systems. Security architects design and implement comprehensive security strategies to protect financial institutions from cyber threats. To succeed in cybersecurity careers, professionals need a strong understanding of network security, encryption, and risk management. Certifications such as Certified Information Systems Security Professional (CISSP) and Certified Ethical Hacker (CEH) can enhance job prospects and demonstrate expertise in the field.

Regtech involves using technology to enhance regulatory compliance and risk management. As financial regulations become more complex, regtech solutions help institutions automate compliance processes, reduce costs, and improve accuracy. Careers in regtech involve developing and implementing technologies that streamline regulatory reporting, transaction monitoring, and risk assessments. Key roles in this field include regtech developers, compliance analysts, and risk management consultants. Regtech developers create software solutions that automate compliance tasks, while compliance analysts ensure that financial institutions adhere to regulatory requirements. Risk management consultants help organizations identify and mitigate risks associated with regulatory compliance. To build a career in regtech, professionals need a strong understanding of financial regulations, programming skills, and experience with compliance processes. Staying informed about regulatory changes and advancements in regtech solutions is crucial for success in this field.

Navigating a career in fintech requires a combination of technical skills, financial knowledge, and adaptability. Pursuing formal education in fields such as finance, computer science, data science, and cybersecurity provides a strong foundation for a career in fintech. Many universities offer specialized programs and courses in fintech, covering topics such as blockchain, AI, and digital banking. Obtaining industry-recognized certifications can enhance job prospects and demonstrate expertise. Certifications such as Certified Financial Analyst (CFA), Certified Information Systems Auditor (CISA), and Certified Blockchain Professional (CBP) are valuable credentials in the fintech industry. Gaining practical experience through internships, cooperative education programs, and entry-level positions is essential for building a successful career in fintech. Internships provide hands-on learning opportunities and help build a professional network. Building a professional network is crucial for career growth in fintech. Attending industry conferences, joining professional organizations, and participating in online forums can help professionals connect with peers, mentors, and potential employers. The fintech industry is constantly evolving, with new technologies and trends emerging regularly. Professionals should commit to continuous learning by staying informed about the latest developments, taking online courses, and reading industry publications.

In addition to technical expertise, soft skills such as communication, problem-solving, and teamwork are essential for success in fintech. Professionals must be able to work effectively with cross-functional teams, communicate complex ideas clearly, and adapt to rapidly changing environments. The fintech industry thrives on innovation and creative problem-solving. Professionals should be open to exploring new ideas, experimenting with emerging technologies, and thinking outside the box to develop innovative solutions. Knowledge of the regulatory environment is crucial in fintech. Professionals must stay informed about regulatory changes and understand how they impact financial institutions and technology solutions. This knowledge helps ensure compliance and mitigates legal risks.

The fintech industry is creating new and emerging career roles that combine finance and technology expertise.

Fintech product managers oversee the development and launch of financial technology products, ensuring they meet customer needs and regulatory requirements. They work closely with development teams, conduct market research, and manage product roadmaps.

    Robo-advisor developers create and maintain the algorithms and platforms that power robo-advisors, ensuring they deliver accurate and personalized recommendations.

    Payment solutions architects design and implement payment systems that facilitate seamless and secure transactions. They work on integrating payment gateways, developing mobile payment solutions, and enhancing user experiences.

AI financial analysts use machine learning algorithms to analyze financial data and generate insights. They develop predictive models for investment strategies, risk assessment, and market analysis.

Blockchain compliance specialists ensure that blockchain projects and cryptocurrency exchanges adhere to regulatory requirements. They conduct compliance audits, develop policies, and monitor transactions for suspicious activity.

Cybersecurity threat hunters proactively search for and identify potential cyber threats within financial systems. They analyze network traffic, investigate anomalies, and develop strategies to prevent cyberattacks.

Regtech consultants advise financial institutions on implementing regulatory technology solutions. They assess compliance needs, recommend appropriate technologies, and assist with deployment and integration.

The fintech industry is poised for continued growth, driven by ongoing technological advancements and increasing demand for innovative financial services. As the industry evolves, new career opportunities will emerge, offering exciting prospects for professionals with the right skills and expertise. Some key trends shaping the future of fintech careers include:

The integration of AI, blockchain, and IoT will create new career opportunities in developing and managing these technologies. Professionals with expertise in these areas will be in high demand. Fintech solutions that promote financial inclusion, such as mobile banking and micro-lending, will drive demand for professionals who can develop and deploy these services in underserved regions. The growing focus on environmental, social, and governance (ESG) factors in finance will create opportunities for professionals who can develop sustainable fintech solutions and assess the ESG impact of financial products. The ongoing digital transformation of financial institutions will require professionals who can manage complex projects, integrate new technologies, and drive organizational change. As cyber threats continue to evolve, there will be a growing need for cybersecurity professionals who can develop innovative solutions to protect financial systems and data. The demand for personalized financial services will drive the development of AI-powered solutions that provide tailored recommendations and experiences. Professionals who can leverage data and AI to create these solutions will be highly sought after.

Navigating a career in finance and technology requires a combination of technical skills, financial knowledge, and adaptability. The fintech industry offers a wide range of career opportunities that combine financial expertise with technological innovation. By pursuing education and training, obtaining certifications, gaining practical experience, and building a professional network, young professionals can build rewarding careers in this dynamic field. The future of fintech careers is bright, with ongoing technological advancements and increasing demand for innovative financial services driving growth. Professionals who stay informed about the latest trends, continuously learn, and embrace innovation will be well-positioned to succeed in the fintech industry. By developing the necessary skills and expertise, young professionals can navigate the complexities of finance and technology and make a meaningful impact on the future of financial services.

17

Conclusion: Shaping the Future of Finance with Technology

Finally, as we come to the end of this deep dive into finance and technology and at the points where they meet, what remains essential is a reflection on the insights of this book and thinking through the future of finance in a digital age. From money and banking to the emergence of fintech, cryptocurrency, and artificial intelligence, each chapter has delved deeply into the vast effect that technology has had in changing the financial landscape. What emerges is a confluence of finance and technology, which will continue to drive innovations in the future; it will disrupt traditional models and democratize access to financial services.

Summarizing the key takeaways

In this book, we have been following the historical evolution of finance, from ancient civilization to today's digital world.

We looked at technology-driven innovations—fintech, blockchain, artificial intelligence—that currently have a profound influence on banking, investing, and financial decisions. From mobile banking potential to algorithmic trading complexities, each chapter has provided a comprehensive overview of key concepts, trends, and challenges that will determine the direction of finance in the future.

We talked about the importance of financial literacy and the work that the regulatory bodies have done to take care of the interests of the consumer and preserve the integrity of the market. We analyzed the ethical considerations that could emanate from algorithmic decision-making and, finally, new risks and opportunities from technologies such as cryptocurrencies and decentralized finance. Real-life case studies, examples, and experienced experts' experiences have made it possible to understand the dynamic drivers changing the financial sector.

Concluding thoughts on the future of finance

As we stand at the crossroads of innovation and disruption, the future of finance holds immense promise and potential. Technology will play a leading role in expanding the outreach of financial services through increased efficiency and help achieve further financial inclusion, from mobile banking applications that empower people to handle their financial lives while on the go to AI-powered investment platforms that serve up personalized advice, this is a series of unlimited possibilities.

But with innovation comes great responsibility. As much as we leverage tech-enabled solutions into our lives, we must take care of the associated risks and challenges. Cybersecurity threats, data privacy concerns, and regulatory complexities need to be handled proactively and collectively to secure financial systems. While we try to get a hold of this confusing digital environment, we should also keep at the back of our minds the ethical consequences our actions and decisions may lead to.

CONCLUSION: SHAPING THE FUTURE OF FINANCE WITH TECHNOLOGY

Encouraging the Youth

What I would like to say to all young people on this journey to anywhere it leads in finance and technology is: be curious. The future belongs to the interested, adaptive, and ready to embrace change. As you experience the challenges now and ahead within the ever-evolving financial frontier, continuously develop and increase your knowledge, looking out for avenues of growth and development.

Embrace lifelong learning as the foundation of your professional journey. Keep up with emerging trends, technological advancements, and best practices in the industry. Use mentorship and guidance by experienced professionals and networking opportunities to broaden your horizons and create meaningful links within the industry. Be guided that success is more than financial; it is the positive impact you will have on the world. Strive to make a difference in other people's lives, either through innovating solutions empowering people, sustainable investment, and social responsibility or ethical choices underpinned with integrity and transparency. In conclusion, the future of finance is bright in light of technology, full of opportunity, and replete with challenges. There is an extreme necessity to understand how these two entities of finance and technology will cross over one another in this fast-evolving world today. Through innovation, lifelong learning, and considerations of ethics, the next generation of financial professionals can drive positive change and lead the way for the industry's future development. With this in mind, let us be adaptive, proactive, and devoted to using technology for better financial services to improve the welfare of society at large.

www.ingramcontent.com/pod-product-compliance
Lightning Source LLC
Chambersburg PA
CBHW071506220526
45472CB00003B/936